smoothies
and other **blended**
drinks

smoothies
and other blended
drinks

elsa petersen-schepelern

photography by
james merrell

TIME
LIFE
BOOKS

Alexandria, Virginia

TIME® LIFE BOOKS

Time-Life Books is a division of Time Life Inc.

TIME LIFE INC.

President and CEO: **George Artandi**

TIME-LIFE CUSTOM PUBLISHING

Vice President and Publisher	**Terry Newell**
Vice President of Sales	
and Marketing	**Neil Levin**
Project Manager	**Jennie Halfant**
Director of Acquisitions	**Jennifer Pearce**
Director of Special Markets	**Liz Ziehl**

Designers	**Penny Stock, Sailesh Patel**
Editor	**Elsa Petersen-Schepelern**,
Production	**Meryl Silbert, Kate MacKillop**
Food Stylist	**Bridget Sargeson**
Stylist	**Ben Kendrick**
Author Photograph	**Francis Loney**

Acknowledgments
My thanks to Norah Meany, Jenny Merrell, Peter Bray, Clare Gordon-Smith, Tessa Kerwood, Louise Sherwin-Stark and Jack Sargeson.

Notes
Take care—not all blenders or food processors are designed to crush ice. If yours isn't, crush the ice separately and spoon into the serving glass before adding the smoothie mixture.
Ice cream scoop measurements used in this book are medium, unless otherwise specified.

TIME-LIFE is a trademark of Time Warner Inc. U.S.A.
Books produced by Time-Life Custom Publishing are available at a special bulk discount for promotional and premium use. Custom adaptations can also be created to meet your specific marketing goals.
Call 1-800-323-5255.

Petersen-Schepelern, Elsa.

    Smoothies and other blended drinks / Elsa Petersen-Schepelern :

with photography by James Merrell

    p.   cm.

CONSTANT Smoothies

Includes index.

ISBN 0-7370-2015-6

1. Blender (Cookery) 2. Smoothies (Beverages) I. Title. II. Title: Smoothies

TX840.B5 P48 1999

641.5'89–dc21   98-52939

                                        CIP

First published in the United Kingdom in 1997 by Ryland Peters & Small, Cavendish House, 51–55 Mortimer Street, London W1N 7TD.
Text copyright © Elsa Petersen-Schepelern 1997.
Design, photographs and illustrations copyright
© Ryland Peters & Small 1997.

Printed and bound in China by Toppan Printing Co.

smoothies and other blended drinks **6**

ice cream smoothies **8**

yogurt drinks **22**

asian flavors **30**

sodas and **crushes 38**

cocktails and coffee **50**

index **64**

smoothies
and other **blended drinks**

Blenders, food processors, and juicers have made life much easier and more exciting for us all. Many different kinds of drinks are quickly assembled using any of these wonder machines. A blender, especially one that is strong enough to crush ice, can be used to mix smoothies, milkshakes, lassi yogurt drinks, and cocktails.

The drinks in this book are quickly made in any of these machines, and are based on the ingredients shown here; ice cream, milk, yogurt, ice, fruit, sugar—as well as wine, spirits, and liqueurs.

If you're watching your weight, you can use low-fat milk and yogurt, as well as fresh fruit juice. Many are so delicious you won't even want to add any sugar at all.

If you're a chili fiend—there's good news! Serve one of the yogurt-based drinks— since capsaicin, the chemical in chilies that makes them hot, is fat soluble rather than water soluble, they'll quell the fires a little and allow you to keep munching!

chocolate mocha milkshake

Coffee and chocolate produces the classic mocha mixture. Make this smoothie stronger or sweeter to taste—heaven for chocoholics!

½ **cup espresso coffee, chilled**

4 oz. semisweet chocolate,

or 2 tablespoons chocolate syrup

3-4 scoops vanilla ice cream

½ **cup cold milk, or to taste**

sugar, to taste

to serve

whipped cream

chocolate curls

ice cream

Purée the coffee and chocolate together in a blender. Add the ice cream and blend again. Add just enough milk to produce the desired consistency, pulse a few times, and add sugar as needed.

Serve topped with a swirl of whipped cream and a sprinkle of chocolate curls.

Serves 1-2

smoothies

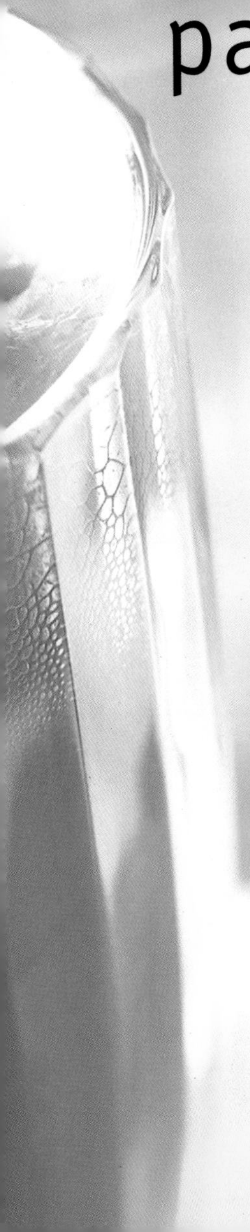

passionfruit
milkshake with grand marnier

Passionfruit with Grand Marnier or Italian Galliano liqueur is a terrific combination. If you like your milkshake even thicker, add extra ice cream: if you like it smoother, add more milk, to taste.

3 passionfruit, chilled

1 tablespoon Grand Marnier or

Italian Galliano liqueur

3 scoops ice cream

½ cup milk, or to taste

sugar, to taste

Scoop the pulp and seeds of 2 passionfruit into the blender, add the Grand Marnier or Galliano, the ice cream, and milk, then blend. Taste, then add sugar and a little extra milk if preferred. Spoon the remaining passionfruit over the top, then serve.

Serves 1–2

A Vienna-coffee-style smoothie—add extra milk if you prefer your coffee creamier, or extra ice cream if you like to stand your spoon up in your coffee!

½ cup espresso coffee, chilled

1 tablespoon Drambuie (optional)

2 scoops vanilla ice cream

½ cup milk, or to taste

sugar, to taste

Place the coffee in a food processor or blender, with the Drambuie, if using. Add the ice cream and half the milk, then blend. Add sugar to taste, and add extra milk if you like your smoothie smoother.

Serves 1–2

coffee ice cream smoothie

ginger shake

If you're a ginger fan, this recipe will be your idea of heaven. Another treat for ginger fiends is what is called a "Ginger Spider" in my native Australia. Place a scoop of ice cream in a soda glass and top with ginger ale. Why a spider? I don't know—but I do know I'm terrified of them!

6 pieces of stem ginger, in syrup

½ cup milk, or to taste

3 scoops ice cream

extra sugar, to taste

to serve (optional)

small scoops of ice cream

extra ginger, chopped

Place the ginger pieces, ice cream, milk, and 6 tablespoons of the syrup in a blender, then purée to a froth. Taste and add extra milk and sugar if preferred. Serve, decorated to taste with another small scoop of ice cream or some extra ginger, chopped.

Serves 1-2

strawberry liqueur smoothie

Old-time American soda jerks were experts, balancing a scoop of ice cream on the edge of the soda glass. If you're not, you could always balance yours on a teaspoon! Make endless variations of this recipe, matching the liqueur to the fruit—Eau de Fraises with strawberries, Poire William with pears, Cassis with blackcurrants, peach liqueur with peaches, or Framboise with raspberries.

A variation on this recipe doesn't even need a blender—make a Strawberry Spider in a tall glass with a scoop of strawberry ice cream, 1 tablespoon of liqueur or strawberry syrup, then top up with soda (preferably strawberry). Pour in the soda very carefully—it will fizz like mad!

8 oz. strawberries

1 tablespoon liqueur, such as Eau de Fraises, Cointreau, or Grand Marnier

3 scoops strawberry ice cream

½ cup milk, or to taste

1 small scoop strawberry ice cream, to serve

Place the first 4 ingredients in a blender and process to a froth. Add extra ice cream for a thicker smoothie, or extra milk, to taste. Serve with a small scoop of ice cream balanced on the edge of the glass.

Serves 1-2

a summer shake with the bright,

sweet scent of ripe berries

passionfruit meringue smoothie

A recipe based on the Pavlova—the national dessert of Australia and New Zealand. It was named in honor of the great Russian ballerina who toured Down Under in the 1920s, when traveling to such frontier territories required a good deal of fortitude.

The Pavlova consists of a large meringue, topped with fresh fruit and whipped cream, then cut into slices like a cake. Passionfruit is almost always included as one of the fruits, plus strawberries in the cooler south of the country and fruits like papaya, mango, and pineapple in the tropical north.

It can be changed according to which fruits are in season and is a particular treat for someone with a sweet tooth. Apply the same seasonal rules to this amazing drink and enjoy yourself!

Make the meringues yourself if you like—but it is much simpler to buy them.

2 small white meringues, about

2 inches in diameter

8 oz. strawberries (or other fruit

in season)

2 passionfruit

3 scoops ice cream, or to taste

½ cup milk, or to taste

to serve (optional)

1 tablespoon whipped cream

pulp and seeds of 1 passionfruit

1 meringue, crumbled

Process the meringues, strawberries, and milk in a blender or food processor.

Add the ice cream and the seeds and pulp of 2 passionfruit. Blend again. Taste and add extra milk if you like a thinner drink, or extra ice cream if you like it thicker.

Pour into tall glasses, and serve, topped with the crumbled meringue, passionfruit pulp, and whipped cream, if using.

Serves 1–2

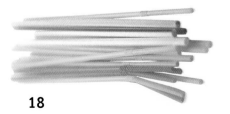

peach melba shake

Another recipe with connections with Down Under. Peach Melba is another of the world's great desserts, created by legendary French chef Escoffier in honor of the 19th century Australian soprano, Dame Nellie Melba—who must have been something of a gourmet, judging by the number of famous dishes named after her. This liquid variation is wonderful at any time of day.

2 poached peaches (canned or homemade)

2 oz. fresh raspberries

3 scoops vanilla ice cream

½ cup milk, or to taste

to serve (optional)

1 tablespoon crushed flaked almonds

1 tablespoon fresh raspberries

whipped cream

If poaching fresh peaches, place them in a saucepan, add 1 tablespoon of sugar per peach, and cover with water or white wine. Bring to a boil and simmer for about 6 to 10 minutes until tender. Cool, slip off the skins, then remove the pits and chill the fruit. Keep the syrup to sweeten the shake.

Place the fruit, ice cream, and milk in a blender or food processor and blend until foaming. Add extra ice cream or extra milk, to taste. Serve, sprinkled with crushed almonds, raspberries, or whipped cream.

Serves 1-2

Overleaf: Peach Melba shake (left) and Passionfruit meringue smoothie (right).

A slimming but filling breakfast—full of flavor, packed with healthy calcium and fiber, and very good for you! If you like your drinks less sweet, reduce the quantity of honey. Other fruit in season, such as berries, can also be substituted. Use chilled fruit to make smoothies—but never put bananas in the refrigerator—or anywhere near citrus fruit—they don't like it. They quickly turn black in the refrigerator, and become over-ripe in a flash if introduced to a citrus fruit.

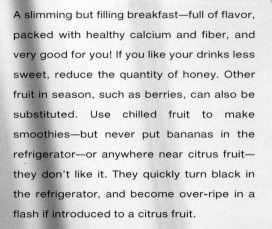

banana and honey
breakfast smoothie

1 cup low-fat milk

1 cup plain low-fat yogurt

½ cup crushed ice

1 tablespoon honey

1 banana

1 tablespoon wheat germ

Place all the ingredients in the blender and process. Add extra fruit if preferred.

Serves 2–4

yogurt drinks

Lassis are a traditional yogurt drink in India, served plain, sweet, or salty—perfect coolers in hot weather. This is a very indulgent form of lassi—but you can take refuge in the fact that yogurt and ginger are very calming for upset stomachs. Use low-fat yogurt if you prefer, and substitute almost any fruit you have on hand, including non-tropical ones like pears, apricots, or peaches. If you use ginger a lot, it's worth making a quantity of purée and keeping it in the refrigerator. Soak 8 oz. of fresh root ginger in water overnight, peel, then purée in a food processor with a little water: it will keep for up to a month.

Place all the ingredients in a blender or food processor and blend. Serve, poured over crushed ice and garnished with mint.

Serves 2-3

flavored yogurt

1 cup peeled, seeded papaya

1 cup crushed pineapple

or pineapple juice

1 banana

1 cup plain yogurt

1 tablespoon puréed fresh ginger

juice and grated zest of 1 lime

to serve

crushed ice

sprigs of mint

tropical fruit lassi
with papaya ginger and lime

drinks are **India's** favorite coolers

vanilla or chocolate
yogurt lassi

Yogurt drinks are traditionally served with hot Indian curries, some of which can be amazingly spicy. Capsaicin, the chemical in chilies that makes them hot, is not water-soluble, so drinking water, alcohol, or tea will not cool your mouth. Milk or yogurt are the perfect antidote, so this is a wonderful drink to serve with any dish containing chilies.

In India, lassis are flavored with rosewater, saffron, pistachio nuts, or spices such as cardamom. Vanilla and chocolate flavors are more familiar to Western tastes, but you could also experiment and create your own.

1⅓ cups plain low-fat yogurt

1⅓ cups low-fat milk

1 cup crushed ice (optional)

1 tablespoon sugar, or to taste

a choice of:

2 tablespoons chocolate syrup,

or a few drops of vanilla extract,

or 1 teaspoon each of rosewater and

crushed cardamom seeds

Blend the yogurt, milk, and crushed ice in a blender or food processor. Add the chosen flavoring and blend again. Taste and add sugar if preferred.

Serves 1–2

Mango, papaya, or banana are perfect fruits to team with milk and yogurt. More unusual is passionfruit and 1 teaspoon Grand Marnier or Galliano liqueur. Milk and yogurt are great sources of calcium—use the low-fat kind if you're watching your waistline.

Yogurt and bananas are good if you have an upset stomach, so you might try this drink as a hangover cure!

The variation below, Savory Yogurt Lassi with Spices, is served as an accompaniment to spicy curry dishes all over India, instead of beer or wine. Salty drinks are very cooling in the searing heat of a true Indian summer!

Variation:

Savory Yogurt Lassi with Spices

Instead of the fruit and sugar listed in the main recipe, substitute 1 teaspoon crushed cumin seeds and salt to taste, then serve.

1 cup plain low-fat yogurt

½ cup low-fat milk

6 large strawberries

choice of fruit, such as:

1 cup raspberries, or

8 oz. apricots or peaches, pitted

sugar, to taste

crushed ice, to serve

Place all the ingredients except the sugar and ice in the blender, and process. Taste, add sugar if preferred, and pour into a glass with crushed ice.

Serves 2-4

fruit salad lassi with strawberries

29

coconut with cloves

To make your own coconut milk, place about 6 tablespoons dried unsweetened coconut in a bowl, and cover with milk or water. Let stand for 20 minutes, then press through a strainer. If you don't want to use coconut milk at all, substitute ordinary milk plus coconut syrup, or any kind of fruit syrup.

½ cup milk

1 cup coconut milk (see above)

3 scoops ice cream

1 teaspoon ground cloves

sugar, to taste

to serve (optional)

crushed ice

finely sliced fresh coconut

Place the milk, coconut milk, ice cream, and cloves in the blender, and process until frothy. Taste and add sugar if required. Blend again until all the sugar has dissolved. Serve poured over crushed ice, topped with finely sliced coconut.

Serves 1–2

asian flavors

pineapple apricot
yogurt smoothie

A recipe with ingredients from opposite ends of India—apricots from the romantic Vale of Kashmir in the shadow of the Himalaya, and pineapples from the tropical south. Use fresh apricots if you like, but I find their sweetness is not to be relied upon.

6 fresh or dried apricots, pitted

1 cup fresh pineapple pieces or

canned unsweetened pineapple

1½ cups plain yogurt

sugar, to taste

to serve

crushed ice

chopped fresh apricot (optional)

If using dried apricots, soak them overnight in cold water to cover.
Blend the pineapple with the apricots and yogurt. Sweeten to taste, then pour over crushed ice.
Serve, topped with chopped apricot, if using.
Serves 2–3

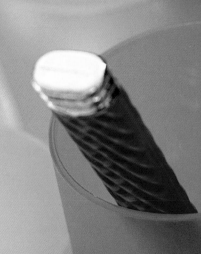

Coconut milk and bananas are a traditional Thai combination—I've added dark rum as an optional extra. The result is a Thailand-meets-the-Caribbean mixture! The mango variation (shown far right, recipe below) can be made with fresh mango, or canned Alphonso mango purée. Usually, I'm not an advocate of using other than fresh produce. However, if you can find canned Alphonso mango in an Asian market, buy it and try it. The Alphonso is famous as the world's greatest mango—and believe me, it is!
Indians are connoisseurs of mangoes—they have hundreds of varieties and use them fresh, cooked, juiced, turned into chutneys, cooked green with meat, served as salads, and in countless other ways.

about 1 cup canned coconut milk

1 cup low-fat milk

2 ripe bananas

1 tablespoon dark rum (optional)

sugar, to taste

crushed ice, to serve

Place all the ingredients in the blender except the sugar and ice. Blend, adding sugar and more rum, to taste. Pour over crushed ice and serve.
Serves 1–2

Variation:

Coconut Milk with Mango
Use 1 cup Alphonso mango purée or 1 large, ripe, fresh mango instead of the bananas and rum. Blend until frothy and serve with a scoop of mango ice cream.

coconut banana shake

great **tropical** ingredients

give the taste of Thailand

pineapple and lime rush

Also delicious made with ice cream rather than yogurt or coconut milk. If keeping cut pineapple in the refrigerator, first wrap it in plastic film to prevent tainting. Fruit varies in sweetness, so taste the crush before serving and add sugar if necessary.

1½ cups plain yogurt or coconut milk

1 cup chopped fresh ripe pineapple

juice and grated rind of 2 limes

1 cup crushed ice

sugar, to taste

to serve (optional)

finely sliced fresh coconut

1 scoop vanilla ice cream

Place the first 4 ingredients in a blender and process. Taste and add sugar if needed. Serve, decorated with the fresh coconut or a scoop of ice cream, if preferred.

Serves 1-2

banana honey and soy milk smoothie

A good breakfast smoothie—full of protein from the soy milk. It is quite sweet, so taste it before you add any extra honey. Other fruits, such as strawberries, bananas, or papaya, can be used instead of the banana.

1 banana

1 teaspoon honey

1 cup soy milk

1 cup crushed ice (optional)

sprigs of mint, to serve (optional)

Place the banana, honey, and soy milk in a blender with the crushed ice, if using, and blend. Serve, topped with sprigs of mint.

Serves 1

orange juice
and strawberry crush

A recipe that can be adapted for any fruit in season—just make sure to chill them all (except the banana). You can process them in a blender, or put them through a juice extractor if you prefer your drink a little smoother. If you use apples, remember to add the orange juice immediately so the apples don't go brown.

1 banana

3 ripe apricots, pitted

6 ripe red strawberries

juice of 1 large orange

3 scoops ice cream

1 cup milk, or to taste

Place all the fruit in the blender with half the milk and blend. Add the ice cream and remaining milk, to taste, and blend again.

Serves 2

sodas and crushes

a perfect summer cooler

zippy with ginger

Indian and Moroccan sharbats are distantly related to the sherbets which are familiar to Westerners. They were introduced by the Moghul emperors who invaded India over its North West Frontier in the 16th century.

If you have a juice extractor, use it to make watermelon juice—though I must admit I prefer the thicker consistency produced by a food processor. You can buy ginger purée in supermarkets, but if you can't find it, just peel fresh ginger root and purée in a food processor with a little water or lemon juice, then freeze in small quantities for future use.

1 small, ripe watermelon, chilled

2 tablespoons ginger purée

(or more, to taste)

water (see method)

sugar, to taste

crushed ice, to serve

watermelon
and ginger
sharbat

Cut the watermelon in wedges, remove and discard the rind and seeds. Blend the flesh in a food processor with the ginger. Add water if the mixture is too thick. Taste and add sugar if needed. Serve over crushed ice.
Serves 2-4

Variation:

Almond Sharbat

Grind 4 oz. skinned almonds in a blender, adding a little water to make a smooth paste. Add a few drops of almond essence (optional), 2 cups water, the crushed seeds from 8 green cardamom pods, 1 teaspoon rosewater (optional) and sugar to taste. Blend, then taste and add more sugar if preferred. Pour over crushed ice and serve.

41

Bananas and limes are typical Southeast Asian ingredients, as is ginger, though not usually in this form. Lychees, if you can find them, make a delicious substitute for the bananas—they are sold either fresh or canned in Asian markets.

2-3 large bananas

grated zest and juice of 2 limes

ginger ale, to taste

crushed ice

sugar, to taste

Purée the bananas in a blender with the lime zest and juice, and a little ginger ale. Taste and add sugar if preferred. Place crushed ice in the bottom of each glass, pour over the mixture, and top up with more ginger ale.
Serves 2

bananas and limes
with ginger ale

pineapple with Jamaican ginger beer

Ginger beer is a favorite drink in Jamaica. Put it together with fresh pineapple, and you have an utterly delicious thirst-quencher—the taste of the Caribbean through a straw! Try it mixed with other fresh fruit too, like very ripe peaches, papayas, or apricots.

3 slices ripe fresh pineapple, chilled

about 1½ cups ginger beer, chilled

about 1 cup crushed ice

Purée the pineapple in a blender with the crushed ice and 2 to 3 tablespoons of ginger beer. Pour into tall glasses and top up with the remaining ginger beer.

Serves 1–2

mint and ginger yogurt soda

Mint and ginger make a gorgeous combination. Ginger purée is sold in some supermarkets—or make it yourself with fresh ginger in a blender. Plain yogurt has a wonderful lemony taste. I must admit I prefer this drink without sugar—so taste it first and decide for yourself.

1½ cups plain low-fat yogurt

leaves from 4 sprigs fresh mint

1-inch piece of root ginger, minced, or 1 tablespoon ginger purée

2 cups soda water, or to taste

sugar, to taste

crushed ice, to serve

Place the yogurt, mint, and ginger in a blender with about ½ cup soda, and blend. Add sugar if preferred. Place crushed ice in the bottom of each glass, pour over the mixture, then top up with soda water.

Serves 2–4

spicy, sweet, and cool—**ginger**, mint, pineapple, and yogurt

Freshly crushed tomato juice is a far cry from the commercial variety. There are many juicers and crushers available now, but if you don't have one, just blend ripe tomatoes in your food processor or blender, then press through a strainer (hard work, but worth it!) Taste the juice before adding any sugar.

Try this recipe if you grow your own fruit, or at the height of summer, when tomatoes are cheap, ripe, and plentiful.

This method can also be used to produce fresh tomato soup (hot or cold), perhaps with a splash of chicken stock, and sprinkled with torn basil leaves. If serving hot, heat the soup just a little, to keep the fresh tomato flavor. To make homemade tomato paste, reduce the pulp over a gentle heat.

2 lb. ripe red plum tomatoes

lemon juice, to taste

salt and pepper, to taste

sugar (optional)

Tabasco sauce (optional)

crushed ice

to serve

sprigs of mint

lemon zest (optional)

Cut the tomatoes into quarters and pass through a juicer. Add lemon juice to keep the color bright, then salt and pepper to taste. Add sugar and Tabasco sauce, if using. Serve with lots of crushed ice, a sprig of mint, and a sprinkle of lemon zest, if using.

Serves 4

homemade
tomato crush

Juicers are wonderful machines. Fresh foaming carrot juice is my favorite—but try this spicy combination too. You could substitute 2 seeded chilies instead of the Tabasco sauce, for a fresh, bright chili taste.

tomato celery and **carrot** crush

2 lb. carrots, chilled

3 stalks celery, chilled

1 lb. tomatoes, chilled

Tabasco sauce, to taste

salt and freshly ground black pepper

crushed ice, to serve

Push the carrots, celery, and tomatoes through a juicer. Alternatively, blend in a food processor with 1 cup iced water, then press through a strainer. Add salt, pepper, and Tabasco, to taste. Serve over crushed ice.

Serves 4-6

campari ruby grapefruit crush

A wonderful drink for a summer brunch party. Serve it as a welcoming drink—one tall glass per person—with a romantic or celebration brunch of toasted brioche with smoked salmon and scrambled eggs garnished with snipped chives. Use ruby grapefruit if you can find them—2 or 3 juicy ones will produce this amount of juice. Serve in a huge glass pitcher so guests can help themselves. Campari isn't very intoxicating, so this is a perfect drink for early in the day—and great as a pre-dinner drink in summer too.

2 cups ruby grapefruit juice, chilled

4 tablespoons Campari, or to taste

crushed ice

sprigs of mint, to serve

Blend 1 cup of crushed ice with the Campari and grapefruit juice. Half-fill a pitcher with more crushed ice, pour in the mixture, cram the top of the jug with mint sprigs and serve.

Serves 2-4

cocktails
and coffee

Grenadine is a beautiful jewel red and made from pomegranates, but you could also use Cointreau, or fresh pomegranate juice, with its slightly bitter taste. (Easy to make—just cut the fruit in half and squeeze over a lemon-squeezer). This is a serious cocktail—if you'd like less alcohol, reduce the quantity of rum and increase the amount of ice—or dilute it with ginger ale.

½ cup crushed pineapple

or pineapple juice

½ cup orange juice

1 cup white rum, or to taste

crushed ice

3 tablespoons Grenadine, Cointreau,

or fresh pomegranate juice, to serve

If using fresh pineapple, peel it first, making sure all the "eyes" are removed, then quarter and core. Pass through a juicer, or blend in a food processor (for a chunkier consistency). Process the pineapple juice, orange juice, rum, and ice in a blender. Serve in chilled glasses, drizzled with Grenadine, Cointreau, or pomegranate juice. Serves 2-4

jamaican rum
punch

The spicy tastes in the traditional Bloody Mary are usually provided by Tabasco sauce. The Food Editor of *Marie Claire* magazine makes her own chili vodka. You could use this instead of the Tabasco for a drink with a bright, clear taste. Test the vodka after 1 day and remove the chili if it's spicy enough. If not, leave for another couple of hours. Take care, and keep tasting, because you can easily make the vodka too hot!

1 cup tomato juice

1 teaspoon Worcestershire sauce

1 tablespoon lemon juice

1 cup crushed ice

1 lemon wedge

1 celery stalk

chili vodka

1 bottle vodka

2 serrano chilies,

halved and seeded

bloody mary with
chili vodka

To make the chili vokda, place the chilies in the bottle of vodka and leave overnight. Taste, leave longer if preferred, then discard the chilies. Keep the vodka in the refrigerator. To make the Bloody Mary, place the tomato juice in a blender with the Worcestershire sauce, lemon juice, 1 measure of chili vodka and the crushed ice. Blend, then pour into tall glasses and serve with a wedge of lemon and a stalk of celery.

Serves 1

Variation:

Not-very-bloody Mary

Omit the vodka and chilies. Add Tabasco, to taste. Proceed as in the main recipe.

fruit-flavored gin makes a
sophisticated cocktail

Place the blueberries in a large glass bottle. Add the sugar and gin, shake well, and set aside for at least 2 weeks, or up to 2 months. Shake the bottle from time to time—you will see the marvelous rich color developing as the days go by.

When ready to serve, place a shot of the gin in a blender with ½ cup crushed ice. Blend and pour into long chilled glasses. Add a sprig of mint and tonic to taste.

Alternatively, serve alone in small aquavit-style glasses. Do not drive!

blueberry gin

Sloe gin is one of the great traditional British Christmas-time drinks. Sloes—the fruit of the blackthorn—are gathered in the hedgerows after the first frosts in fall, then placed in bottles with gin and sugar, and set aside until Christmas. I think it should be drunk in small glasses—it tastes wonderful, but is very strong, and can be something of a trap. Blueberry gin is a variation on a theme. Serve it straight in small glasses—or in long ones with ice and tonic water. Delicious and the most marvelous color!

1 cup blueberries

6 tablespoons sugar

1 large bottle (750 ml) gin

to serve (optional)

crushed ice

tonic water

sprigs of mint

coffee frappé

A wonderful pick-me-up on a hot summer afternoon—and one that can be adapted to other ingredients, such as tomato juice, orange and raspberry juice, pear or apricot nectar, crushed pineapple with some extra juice added, and so on.

6 tablespoons freshly ground coffee

4 cups boiling water

sugar, to taste

to serve (optional)

¼ cup whipped cream

2 oz. shaved semisweet chocolate

Put the coffee in a French press coffee pot and add boiling water. Leave for 3 minutes, pour into a pitcher with sugar to taste. It should be sweeter than you would usually like. Cool, then freeze in a shallow plastic tray. When solid but not rock-hard, process in a blender, then pour into cups or glasses. Top with cream and chocolate, or serve plain.

Serves 6

white rum and fresh mango
—a great **tropical** cocktail

Use white rum in this recipe for a pretty, clear summer look. However, I grew up in the tropics and I much prefer dark rum; I would always use it instead. New Zealand food writer Clare Ferguson has come up with a marvelous rum idea—keep 2 vanilla beans in a bottle of rum and use it in drinks and for cooking. It smells like the very best rum and raisin ice cream!

1 large ripe mango

juice of 1 lemon

½ cup white rum

(or dark if preferred)

sugar, for glass

crushed ice

Peel the mango and slice the flesh into a blender. Add the lemon juice, rum, and 1 cup crushed ice, then blend.

Rub the cut lemon around the rim of a glass and press into sugar. Place more crushed ice in the glass and pour over the crush.

Serves 1

mango and rum crush

61

thick tropical crush

This tropical crush is so thick and wonderful it's almost a soup. It will serve one person as a smoothie, and about six people as a champagne cocktail. Don't forget to chill all the fruits first—but wrap up any aromatic ones in plastic wrap to prevent tainting.

tropical fruits such as:

8 oz. cubed fresh papaya

1 cup cubed fresh pineapple

chilled champagne (see method)

sugar, to taste (optional)

watermelon pieces, to serve

Process the fruits in the blender with ½ cup champagne. Add sugar to taste, if using. Pour into a chilled glass, and serve with the watermelon. Alternatively, divide between 6 glasses, top with champagne, and serve as champagne cocktails.

Serves 1 or 6

62

Index

A
almond sharbat 41
apricot, pineapple yogurt
    smoothie 32

B
bananas 22, 29
    coconut banana shake 34
    and honey breakfast
        smoothie 22
    honey, soy milk smoothie 36
    and limes with gingerale 42
bloody Mary with chili vodka 54
blueberry gin 57

C
Campari ruby grapefruit 50
Caribbean 34, 44
carrot, celery, and tomato
    crush 49
champagne 62
chilies 6, 49. 54
chili vodka 54
chocolate
    mocha milkshake 8
    lassi 27
coconut
    banana shake 34
    with cloves 30
    dried 30
    milk 30, 36
    milk with banana shake 34
coffee
    frappé 58
    ice cream smoothie 12
crushes
    celery, tomato, and carrot 49
    homemade tomato 46
    mango and rum 61
    orange juice strawberry 38
    pineapple with Jamaican
        ginger beer 40
    pineapple and lime 36
    thick tropical 62

F
frappé
    apricot nectar 58
    coffee 58
    orange and raspberry 58
    pear nectar 58
    pineapple, crushed 58

tomato juice 58
fruit salad lassi 29

G
Galliano 11, 29
gin, blueberry 57
ginger
    ale, banana and lime with 42
    beer, pineapple with
        Jamaican 44
    mint and, yogurt soda 44
    purée, making 24, 41, 44
    shake 14
    tropical fruit lassi with 24
    watermelon and, sharbat 41
Grand Marnier 11, 29
grapefruit, Campari ruby 50

H
homemade tomato crush 46
honey
    banana and, breakfast
        smoothie 22
    honey soy milk smoothie 36

I
ice cream smoothie, coffee 12
India 24, 27, 29, 32, 41

J
Jamaican
    ginger beer, pineapple with 44
    rum punch 53

L
lassis 6
    fruit salad with strawberries 29
    pineapple apricot yogurt 32
    savory yogurt with spices 29
    tropical fruit lassi with 24
    vanilla or chocolate 27
lime
    bananas and, with gingerale
        42
    tropical fruit lassi 24
liqueurs and spirits
    bloody Mary with chili vodka
    Campari ruby grapefruit 50
    Cassis 16
    Cointreau 53
    Eau de Fraises 16
    Framboise 16
    Galliano 11
    Grand Marnier 11
    Grenadine 53

Jamaican rum punch 53
mango and rum crush 61
Poire William 16
peach 16
vodka, chili 54

M
mango 29, 34
    coconut milk with, shake 34
    and rum crush 61
Melba shake, peach 19
meringue 18
milkshakes
    chocolate mocha 8
    ginger shake 14
    passionfruit with Galliano 11
mint and ginger yogurt soda 44
mocha milkshake, chocolate 8

N
not-very-bloody Mary 54

O
orange juice and strawberry
    crush 38

P
papayas 24, 29, 62
    tropical fruit lassi with 24
passionfruit
    meringue smoothie 18
    milkshake 11
peach melba shake 19
pineapple, 62
    apricot yogurt smoothie 32
    with Jamaican ginger beer
        44
    and lime crush 36
pistachio nuts 27
punch, Jamaican rum 53

R
rosewater 27
rum
    mango and, crush 61
    Jamaican rum punch 53

S
savory yogurt lassi 29
shakes
    coconut banana 34
    coconut milk with mango 34
    peach Melba 19
sharbat
    almond 41

watermelon and ginger 41
smoothies
    banana and honey breakfast
        22
    banana honey soy milk 36
    coffee ice cream 12
    passionfruit meringue 18
    pineapple apricot yogurt 32
    strawberry liqueur 16
sodas
    bananas and limes with
        ginger ale 42
    mint and ginger yogurt 44
    soy milk, banana, honey and,
        smoothie 36
spider
    ginger 15
    strawberry 16
spirits, see liqueurs and spirits
strawberries 16
    fruit salad lassi with 29
    orange juice and, crush 38
    strawberry liqueur smoothie 16

T
thick tropical crush 62
tomato
    bloody Mary 54
    celery, carrot and, crush 49
    crush, homemade 46
    not-very-bloody Mary 54
tropical fruit lassi with papaya,
    ginger and lime 24

V
vanilla or chocolate yogurt lassi
    27
vodka, chili 54

W
watermelon 62
    and ginger sharbat 41

Y
yogurt 6
yogurt drinks
    banana and honey breakfast
        smoothie 22
    fruit salad lassi 29
    mint and ginger soda 44
    pineapple apricot smoothie 32
    pineapple and lime crush 36
    savory yogurt lassi 29
    tropical fruit lassi 24
    vanilla or chocolate lassi 27

Me • I'm Yours Forever • Love & Kisses • My
Love & Kisses • I Love You • You're • My
es • I Love You • You're Mine • Be My Valentine • I
e • I'm Yours Forever • Love & Kisses • I Love You
One and Only • I Love You Truly • Kiss Me • Be My
Me • I'm Yours Forever • Love & Kisses • You're My
Love & Kisses • I Love You • You're Mine • Be My
es • I Love You • You're Mine • Be My Valentine • I
e • I'm Yours Forever • Love & Kisses • I Love You
One and Only • I Love You Truly • Kiss Me • Be My
Me • I'm You Kisses • You're My
Love & Kiss u're Mine • Be My
es • I Love Y Be My Valentine •
e • I'm You Kisses • I Love You
One and Only Kiss Me • Be My
Me • I'm You Kisses • You're My
Love & Kiss u're Mine • Be My
es • I Love You • You're Mine • Be My Valentine •

I Love You • You're Mine • Be My Valentine • Kiss
One and Only • I Love You Truly • I'm Yours Forever
Valentine • Kiss Me • I'm Yours Forever • Love & K
You're My One and Only • I Love You Truly • Kiss
Truly • I'm Yours Forever • Love & Kisses • You're M
I Love You • You're Mine • Be My Valentine • Kiss
One and Only • I Love You Truly • I'm Yours Forever
Valentine • Kiss Me • I'm Yours Forever • Love & K
You're My One and Only • I Love You Truly • Kiss
Truly • I'm Yours Forever • Love & Kisses • You're M
I Love You • You're Mine • Be My Valentine • Kiss
One and Only • I Love You Truly • I'm Yours Forever
Valentine • Kiss Me • I'm Yours Forever • Love & K
You're My One and Only • I Love You Truly • Kiss
Truly • I'm Yours Forever • Love & Kisses • You're M
I Love You • You're Mine • Be My Valentine • Kiss
One and Only • I Love You Truly • I'm Yours Forever
Valentine • Kiss Me • I'm Yours Forever • Love & K

Baked from the Heart

Baked from the Heart

Heart

GIFTS OF LOVE FOR SPECIAL OCCASIONS

RECIPES & STYLING BY

Stephanie Greenleigh

PHOTOGRAPHY BY

Kathryn Kleinman

CONCEIVED & PRODUCED BY

Jennifer Barry Design

A Kirsty Melville Book

Ten Speed Press
Box 7123, Berkeley, California 94707

Distributed in Canada by Publishers Group West, in New Zealand
by Tandem Press, in South Africa by Real Books, in India by Maya Publishers Pvt Ltd.,
and in the United Kingdom and Europe by Airlift Books.

Concept and Design: Jennifer Barry Design, Sausalito, California
Editor: Val Cipollone
Design and Production Assistant: Kristen Wurz
Photography Assistant: Caroline Kopp
Photography Production Assistant: Teresa Retzlaff
Food Stylist Assistants: Susan Snider and Claudia Breault

Library of Congress Cataloging-in-Publication Data
Greenleigh, Stephanie.
Baked from the heart : gifts of love for special occasions /
recipes and styling by Stephanie Greenleigh; photos by Kathryn Kleinman;
produced by Jennifer Barry Design.
p.   cm.
Includes index.
ISBN 0-89815-938-5 (cloth)
1. Baking.   I. Title.
TX763.G653 1997
641.8'15--dc21   97-20706   CIP

Printed in Hong Kong

First printing, 1997

1 2 3 4 5 6 7 8 9 10 — 01 00 99 98 97

For the two most important women in my life,
my mother and my grandmother, Clara, and for my daughter,
the budding baker, Elise Marie

Contents

INTRODUCTION 8

TIPS FOR BAKING & DECORATING 14

COOKIES 19

CAKES & TARTS 43

QUICK BREADS & PASTRIES 65

EGGS & BATTERS 79

BAKER'S NOTES 103

METRIC CONVERSIONS 107

RESOURCES 108

ACKNOWLEDGMENTS 109

INDEX 110

I can still   remember
racing home from school   with my sister, bursting
through the front door, and seeing what my mother had
prepared for George Washington's birthday. There it was! A table
lying in wait, set with patriotic red placemats, and decorated
with a seasonal centerpiece of cherry blossoms. The menu, from
my mother's point of view, was prepared to suit such
a stately occasion: pork chops, peas, and Tater Tots.®
The dessert, memorable, was cherry Jell-O®
and whipped cream tunneled into a
high-rising angel food cake.
There was no question in
my mind: I knew
she loved
us.

8

Special occasions were a big deal at our house. And with almost every holiday acknowledged, there were many. Invariably, my mom put as much effort into presentation as she did preparation. She planned creatively, and the kitchen was her headquarters. She had a knack for making all the work and anticipation as much a celebration as the occasion itself. As I've gotten older, now having kids of my own, I've come to appreciate my mom's time and effort as the generous gifts they were.

In our household, despite the sometimes frantic juggling of careers, kids, and carpools, the kitchen is still the hub, especially when preparing for a certain occasion. I believe baking from scratch is one of the simplest and most thoughtful ways to make a celebration special. This is a collection of recipes, from the quick and easy to the elaborate, for that rare occasion when you do have the luxury of taking your time and getting all the details right. You can tell your partner how much you care by baking him or her a decadent chocolate torte, or thank a neighbor for running the kids to baseball practice with some apple turnovers. Celebrate special occasions, big or small, with handmade gifts from the kitchen.

I make my career as a food stylist and, looking back over my mother's influence, this seems a very natural progression. I've included some of the baking and decorating techniques I find helpful for getting the most out of the time I spend in the kitchen. Some of the how's and why's of good baking and styling are spelled out in a section called Tips for Baking & Decorating. More often than not, a simple cake or cookies can be made to look special by using decorative molds or holiday-inspired cutters. Forgoing special equipment, you can make plain baked goods beautiful by decorating them with a heart-shaped stencil, tying them with a silk ribbon, or putting them in a pretty box decorated with greens and flowers from your garden. Like mom said, "Think presentation!"

In preparation for special occasions, Mexican woman will cook for days, making a particular *mole* or baking dozens of their famous wedding cakes. For them, the preparation is an important part of the celebration. They have a saying, *panza llena, corazón contento,* "a full stomach is a contented heart." I try to bring the same philosophy into my kitchen, inviting others to help and, in doing so, share in the fun. Savory or sweet, the unwritten ingredients in these recipes are the time, effort, and love that bring food to life.

ABOVE AND RIGHT:
Package pretty homemade cookies in
decorated envelopes, boxes, and bags.

Tips for Baking & Decorating

These are some of my tried and true techniques for creating professional-looking baked goods. I have also included a list of my favorite tools.

TIPS

Decorating with Royal Icing: First, set up a decorating area where you will have plenty of room to work. I like to put down a plastic tablecloth to catch any icing spills. You should have a tray containing cosmetic swabs, 2-inch squares of paper towels, long-handled tweezers, an assortment of a paintbrushes, toothpicks, and an empty egg carton or mini-muffin tray filled with various edible decorations. Your bowls containing colored icing and filled pastry bags should be easily accessible. Keep a damp towel (for sticky fingers) by your side.

In most cases, Royal Icing mixed according to my recipe is what you will be working with—the type you use for piping detailed decoration. In those cases where both detailed decoration and a background are called for, you will need both the original recipe and a thinner version. Always start with your background and your thinned icing, which should be the consistency of heavy cream. This can be made by adding a few drops of warm water to the original recipe. Using a pastry bag fitted with a number 5 tube, outline the cookie's shape, leaving a 1/4-inch border around the perimeter. Pipe another line of icing, just inside and touching the previous, until the whole surface of the cookie is covered. The icing will spread on its own, forming a smooth and durable surface. Once the surface is set, switch to the original icing, and detail the cookie.

Mistakes happen. For instance, you have spent a good deal of time piping in the background icing. It has dried to a perfectly smooth surface and you have just finished the last letter, in beautifully intricate script, of your valentine's name. But instead of looking like an "e," it looks like an "s." How do you save this cookie? Using a toothpick, quickly pick up what you can of the "e." Dip a cosmetic swab in cold water and dab the surface to remove all traces of the misshapen letter. With a small paintbrush lightly brush the area to smooth over the surface icing. Let the area dry completely and try your letter again.

Freezing cutout cookie dough: When using an intricate cookie mold or cutter, freeze the shaped cookie dough for five minutes before you bake it. This sets the surface design and shape, insuring picture-perfect cookies.

Handling delicate dough: To roll out and cut particularly thin (1/8 inch) or fragile cookie dough, I recommend rolling it out on a piece of parchment paper fitted to the size of your cookie sheet. Using floured cookie cutters, mark shapes in the dough on the parchment, spacing them about 2 inches apart. Remove the excess dough from in between the shapes, and transfer the parchment, with the shaped dough on top, onto the cookie sheet. Gather the excess dough and continue working on parchment until all the dough is used.

Piping with a pastry bag: You may want to practice on a piece of waxed or parchment paper, particularly if you are trying a new decoration or design. For piping letters or an intricate decoration, I find a #2 plain round tube works best. Place the filled pastry bag in the palm of your writing hand. Using your other hand as a guide, and holding the bag at a 45-degree angle, lightly touch the tube to the surface of the cake or cookie. With even pressure, squeeze the pastry bag, forming the design just *above* the surface. When finishing a line or letter, stop squeezing the bag and lift the tube away from the baked good.

If you are piping with different tubes, using a coupler can make the job a lot easier. To use a coupler, unscrew the nut, sometimes called a "ring," and put the coupler pointed side down into the pastry bag, making sure the threads are pulled down through the narrow end of the bag. Put a decorating tube over the coupler and screw the nut back on. Fill the bag and pipe as needed. To change piping tubes, unscrew the nut, change the tube, and screw the nut back into place.

Preparing decorative molds and cake pans: Brush decorative molds and cake pans with slightly cooled melted butter, taking care to coat them completely, including all the crevices. Then, dust them with flour, tapping out the excess. This process insures your baked cakes will release easily, without sticking to the mold or pan.

Whipping egg whites: To ensure perfectly whipped egg whites, use a stainless steel mixing bowl and a beater that have been cleaned with salt and hot water and thoroughly dried.

TOOLS

Baking sheets: Buy the best and heaviest your budget allows. I prefer insulated stainless steel baking sheets, as they promote even baking and do not warp in the oven.

Metal spatulas: For smoothly spreading glaze or to decoratively swirl whipped cream, nothing comes close to a good spatula. My collection contains various sizes from a 1-inch pâté spreader to a 10-inch icing spatula. My favorite little spatula is an artist's palette knife, which can be purchased at art supply shops.

Parchment paper: I consider this purchase as important as using quality ingredients. Although many cookbooks claim that waxed paper can be substituted, I find the strength and texture of parchment superior. Parchment allows baked goods to be removed easily from their pans, limiting breakage of delicate goods. In a pinch, parchment can also be used to make a paper cone for piping icing.

Pastry bags: When working with several different colors of icing, I find using disposable polypropylene pastry bags is a great help. These bags can be fitted with your favorite pastry tubes for a variety of designs. Another helpful item is the coupler. This apparatus allows you to interchange decorating tubes while working with the same bag of icing.

ABOVE AND RIGHT:
Heart-shaped cookie cutters, decorated note cards, and pretty ribbon ties can be used when wrapping gifts and setting tables for many occasions.

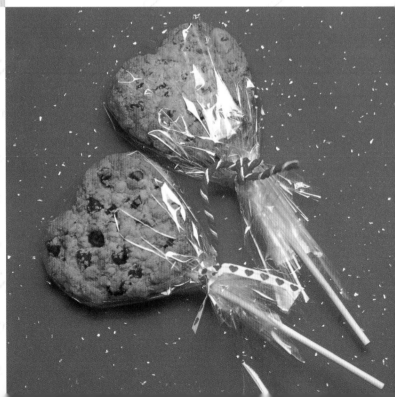

Cookies

VANILLA SUGAR COOKIES

GINGERBREAD COOKIES

CHOCOLATE PEPPERMINT SHORTBREAD

LINZER COOKIES

NEW YEAR'S FORTUNE COOKIES

MERINGUE & CHOCOLATE KISSES

GINGER LIME BARS

ISCHLERS

PINE NUT WEDDING HEARTS

CHOCOLATE PEANUT BUTTER LOLLIPOPS

Menu for a Cookie Decorating Party

VANILLA SUGAR COOKIES

GINGERBREAD COOKIES

CHOCOLATE PEPPERMINT SHORTBREAD

HOT SPICED APPLE CIDER

HOT COCOA WITH WHIPPED CREAM

COFFEE

21

Vanilla Sugar Cookies

Early spring blossoms laced with decorated cookies make a very special valentine. These crisp buttery cookies are the perfect canvas for a palette of spring colors.

1³/4 cups flour
2 teaspoons baking powder
³/4 teaspoon ground cinnamon
Pinch of salt
¹/2 cup unsalted butter, at room temperature
¹/2 cup granulated sugar
¹/2 cup firmly packed light brown sugar
1 large egg, at room temperature
1 teaspoon vanilla extract
1 teaspoon finely grated orange zest

ROYAL ICING
4 teaspoons powdered egg whites
¹/4 cup warm water
1 tablespoon freshly squeezed lemon juice
3¹/2 cups sifted confectioners' sugar
2 drops glycerin

Line two baking sheets with parchment paper. In a mixing bowl, whisk together the flour, baking powder, cinnamon, and salt, and set aside.

Cream the butter and sugars with an electric mixer set on medium speed until light and fluffy. Beat in the egg, vanilla extract, and orange zest. On low speed, gradually beat in the dry ingredients until well combined. Divide the dough in half, flatten into disks, wrap tightly, and refrigerate until firm, about 1 hour.

Heat the oven to 325°. Working between two pieces of parchment paper, roll a disk of dough to an ¹/8-inch thickness. With floured 2- to 3-inch heart-shaped cookie cutters, cut out shapes and freeze them (see Tips for Baking & Decorating, page 14). Bake the cookies until the edges are lightly browned, 12 to 15 minutes. Transfer the cookies to wire racks and let them cool completely. Continue shaping and baking the cookies until all the dough is used.

To make the Royal Icing: Beat the powdered egg whites and water with an electric mixer set on low speed until all the water is absorbed, about 2 minutes. Add the lemon juice and gradually beat in the confectioners' sugar until stiff, but not dry. Add the glycerin and beat 1 minute more. Once cool, decorate the cookies with Royal Icing. *Makes 36 cookies*

Note: Edible paints (luminescent powders you mix with water) can be used to color the Royal Icing, though food coloring can be used as well. Edible paints, powdered egg whites, and glycerin are all available in baking supply shops or from catalogs (page 108).

Spring blossoms and cookies
decorated in a palette of pastel colors make
a very special valentine. Be sure to anchor
the branches in the bottom of
the vase with florists' foam to balance
the weight of the cookies.

Gingerbread Cookies

These gingerbread cookies are as wonderful to look at as they are to eat. The stiffness of the dough makes them particularly easy to mold. To make an edible ornament, string a ribbon through a hole in the top of each cookie.

3 cups flour
1 teaspoon baking powder
2 teaspoons pumpkin pie spice
1/2 teaspoon salt
1/4 cup unsalted butter, at room temperature

1/2 cup firmly packed light brown sugar
1 large egg, at room temperature
1/2 cup light molasses
1 teaspoon vanilla extract

Line a baking sheet with parchment paper. Prepare a ceramic cookie mold according to the manufacturer's instructions. In a mixing bowl, whisk together the flour, baking powder, pumpkin pie spice, and salt, and set aside.

Cream the butter and sugar with an electric mixer set on medium speed until light and fluffy. Beat in the egg, molasses, and vanilla. On low speed, gradually beat in the dry ingredients until well combined. Flatten the dough into a disk, wrap tightly, and refrigerate until firm, at least 2 hours.

Heat the oven to 325°. Shape the cookies with the cookie mold according to the manufacturer's instructions. Transfer the cookies to the baking sheet and freeze them (see Tips for Baking & Decorating, page 14). Bake the cookies until the edges are lightly browned, 10 to 15 minutes. Transfer the cookies to wire racks and let them cool completely. *Makes 8 cookies*

Note: To shape cookies with cookie cutters, on a lightly floured board, roll the dough to a 1/4-inch thickness. With floured cookie cutters, cut out shapes, and transfer them to a baking sheet. Bake as directed. To make holes in the tops of the cookies, pierce them with a wooden skewer or toothpick just after removing them from the oven.

Chocolate Peppermint Shortbread

Chocolate combined with peppermint make these shortbread cookies an irresistible treat.
Package them in a gift box and send them to a favorite friend.

3 cups flour

2 teaspoons baking powder

$1/2$ teaspoon salt

$1/2$ cup unsalted butter, at room temperature

1 cup granulated sugar

1 large egg, at room temperature

3 ounces cream cheese, at room temperature

2 ounces unsweetened chocolate, melted and cooled

1 teaspoon vanilla extract

1 teaspoon peppermint extract

1 recipe Royal Icing (page 22)

Line two baking sheets with parchment paper. In a mixing bowl, whisk together the flour, baking powder, and salt, and set aside.

Cream the butter and sugar with an electric mixer set on medium speed until light and fluffy. Beat in the egg, cream cheese, chocolate, and vanilla and peppermint extracts. On low speed, gradually beat in the dry ingredients until well combined (the dough will be fairly sticky). Divide the dough into 4 pieces, flatten into disks, wrap tightly, and refrigerate until firm, at least 2 hours.

Heat the oven to 350°. On a lightly floured board, roll a disk of dough, adding flour as necessary, to a $1/4$-inch thickness. With a floured 3-inch heart-shaped cookie cutter, cut out shapes and freeze them (see Tips for Baking & Decorating, page 14). Bake the cookies until the edges are lightly browned, 12 to 15 minutes. Transfer the cookies to wire racks and let them cool completely. Continue shaping and baking the cookies until all the dough is used. Once cool, decorate the cookies with Royal Icing. *Makes 36 cookies*

Linzer Cookies

Reminiscent of stained glass, colorful fruit fillings shine through rich pastry windows. Tuck these beautiful cookies into a Christmas stocking or leave them out for Santa to eat.

2 1/3 cups flour
2/3 cup finely chopped hazelnuts
1/8 teaspoon salt
1 cup unsalted butter, at room temperature
1 cup confectioners' sugar

2 large egg yolks, at room temperature
1 teaspoon vanilla extract
1 cup apricot, plum, or strawberry fruit preserves
or fruit butter

Line two baking sheets with parchment paper. In a mixing bowl, whisk together the flour, nuts, and salt, and set aside.

Cream the butter and sugar with an electric mixer set on medium speed until light and fluffy. Beat in the egg yolks and vanilla extract. On low speed, gradually beat in the dry ingredients until well combined. Divide the dough in half. Flatten the dough into disks, wrap tightly, and refrigerate until firm, about 1 hour.

Heat the oven to 325°. On a lightly floured board, roll a disk of dough to an 1/8-inch thickness. With floured 3- to 4-inch cookie cutters, cut out shapes. With a smaller cookie cutter, cut out a "window" from half the shapes. Freeze all the shapes (see Tips for Baking & Decorating, page 14). Bake the cookies until firm, 12 to 15 minutes. They will be fairly pale in color. Transfer the cookies to wire racks and let them cool completely. Continue shaping and baking cookies until all the dough is used.

To assemble the cookies: Using a small spatula, spread the top of each windowless cookie with about 1 teaspoon preserves. Top with the remaining cookies, bottom sides down, forming sandwiches. If the cookies are not eaten soon after making, store them, airtight, in the refrigerator. *Makes 20 sandwiches*

Note: Fruit butters have intense flavor and work very well here. They are, however, not as colorful as fruit preserves.

New Year's Fortune Cookies

Hide romantic fortunes for someone special to find inside these homemade cookies.
What better way is there to start the new year?

2/3 cup flour
1/4 cup almonds, toasted and ground
1/8 teaspoon salt
3 large egg whites, at room temperature

1 cup granulated sugar
1/2 cup unsalted butter, melted
1/8 teaspoon almond extract
24 prepared fortunes, cut into 3-inch strips

Heat the oven to 325°. Brush two baking sheets with butter. Sift together the flour, almonds, and salt, and set aside.

Whisk the egg whites, sugar, melted butter, and almond extract by hand until well combined. Add the dry ingredients, and stir until the batter is smooth. The batter will be fairly loose. Drop 1 tablespoonful of batter for each cookie onto a baking sheet. The batter will spread in baking, so space tablespoonfuls at least 3 inches apart. Bake until the edges of the cookies are light golden brown, 10 to 12 minutes.

To shape the cookies: Working quickly, remove a cookie from a baking sheet with a metal spatula. Fold the cookie in half around a prepared fortune. Make the second fold by holding the two ends of the cookie over the rim of a glass and pushing them down. Place the fortune cookies in a muffin tin to hold their shape. Let them cool completely. Continue baking and shaping the cookies until all the batter is used. *Makes 24 cookies*

Desires are nourished by delays.

Meringue & Chocolate Kisses

I think George Washington would have been happy to mix cherries and chocolate. Here, cherry syrup colors and flavors
a billowy cloud of meringue, kissed with bittersweet chocolate

3 large egg whites, at room temperature
1 cup superfine sugar
1/2 teaspoon cream of tartar
2 plus 1/2 teaspoons cherry syrup

2 drops red food coloring (optional)
6 ounces bittersweet chocolate
1 tablespoon vegetable oil

Heat the oven to 275°. Line a baking sheet with parchment paper.

Beat the egg whites with an electric mixer set on medium speed just until broken up, about 1 minute. Gradually beat in the sugar and cream of tartar while slowly increasing mixing speed. Add 2 teaspoons cherry syrup and red food coloring and beat on high speed just until stiff peaks form. The egg whites will be stiff and glossy, but should not be dry.

Drop the egg whites by generous teaspoonfuls onto the baking sheet. With a spoon, shape the egg whites into 1 1/2-inch mounds, making a depression in the center of each. Bake the meringues for 15 minutes. Without removing them from the oven, turn the oven off and prop the door open slightly. Let the meringues sit in the oven until completely dry, about 30 minutes. Transfer them to a wire rack and let them cool completely.

In the meantime, make the chocolate filling. In a double boiler, melt the chocolate and the oil over low heat, stirring frequently until smooth. Remove the pan from the heat, let the mixture cool to room temperature, and stir in 1/2 teaspoon cherry syrup. Spoon the filling into the depressions made in the meringues. Transfer the meringues to wire racks and let sit until the filling is set. *Makes 24 meringues*

Ginger Lime Bars

An exotic version of the old-fashioned favorite, lemon bars, these tangy-sweet confections are perfect for a summertime picnic.

PASTRY
2 cups flour
1/2 cup confectioners' sugar
1/4 teaspoon salt
1/2 teaspoon ground ginger
1 cup butter, chilled

FILLING
1/4 cup flour
1 teaspoon baking powder
4 large eggs, at room temperature
1 1/2 cups confectioners' sugar
1 tablespoon finely grated lime zest
1/3 cup freshly squeezed lime juice
Confectioners' sugar, for dusting

Heat the oven to 350°.

To make the pastry crust: In a mixing bowl, sift together the flour, sugar, salt, and ginger. Cut the butter into the dry ingredients with a pastry cutter until the mixture resembles coarse meal. Pat the crumbs, in an even layer, into a 13 x 9-inch baking dish. Bake the crust until lightly browned, about 20 minutes. Transfer the crust to a rack and let it cool slightly.

To make the filling: In a mixing bowl, sift together the flour and baking powder, and set aside. Beat the eggs with an electric mixer set on medium speed until pale. Gradually beat in the sugar until well combined. Beat in the lime zest and juice. On low speed, gradually beat in the dry ingredients just until the batter is evenly mixed.

Spread the filling over the crust, return it to the oven, and bake until the filling is set, 20 to 25 minutes more. Transfer the dish to a wire rack and let it cool completely. Generously dust the pastry with confectioners' sugar and cut it into bars.
Makes 36 bars

Ischlers

An elegant teatime cookie originating in old Vienna, this version sandwiches tart lingonberries and cream cheese between rich, buttery wafers. A chocolate glaze completes the package. They are delightful served with a cup of Earl Grey tea.

2 cups flour
1 cup finely ground walnuts
$^1/_8$ teaspoon salt
1 cup unsalted butter, at room temperature
$^3/_4$ cup granulated sugar
1 large egg, at room temperature
1 teaspoon vanilla extract
1 recipe Chocolate Glaze (pages 59–60)

FILLING

4 ounces cream cheese, at room temperature
1 tablespoon plus 1 teaspoon lingonberries in syrup, drained
$^1/_4$ teaspoon vanilla extract

Line two baking sheets with parchment paper. Sift together the flour, ground nuts, and salt, and set aside.

Cream the butter and sugar with an electric mixer set on medium speed until light and fluffy. Beat in the egg and vanilla extract. On low speed, gradually beat in the dry ingredients until well combined. Divide the dough into 4 pieces, flatten into disks, wrap tightly, and refrigerate until firm, at least 1 hour.

In the meantime, make the filling. Beat the cream cheese and lingonberries with an electric mixer set on medium speed until light and fluffy. Beat in the vanilla extract. Refrigerate the filling until ready to use.

Heat the oven to 325°. On a lightly floured board, roll a disk of dough to an $^1/_8$-inch thickness. With a floured 2-inch cookie cutter, cut out shapes and freeze them (see Tips for Baking & Decorating, page 14). Bake the cookies until firm, 12 to 15 minutes. They will be pale in color. Transfer the cookies to wire racks and let them cool completely. Continue shaping and baking the cookies until all the dough is used.

To assemble the cookies: Using a small spatula, spread half of the cookies with about 1 teaspoon filling. Top with remaining cookies, bottom sides down, forming sandwiches. Dip half of each sandwich into the Chocolate Glaze. Transfer the cookies to wire racks until the glaze is cool and set, about 15 minutes. If the cookies are not eaten soon after making, store, airtight, in the refrigerator. *Makes 20 sandwiches*

Pine Nut Wedding Hearts

This is my own variation on Mexican Wedding Cakes, special confections made for celebrating an engagement or wedding. These cookies are particularly elegant, worth the extra effort it takes to make them.

2 cups flour
1/4 teaspoon salt
1 cup unsalted butter, at room temperature
1/4 cup granulated sugar

1/4 cup confectioners' sugar
1 teaspoon vanilla extract
3 ounces pine nuts, toasted and finely chopped
Confectioners' sugar, for dusting

Heat the oven to 325°. Line two baking sheets with parchment paper. Fit a cookie press with a 1/4-inch round tip. Sift together the flour and salt, and set aside.

Cream the butter and the sugars with an electric mixer set on medium speed until light and fluffy. Beat in the vanilla extract. On low speed, gradually beat in the dry ingredients until well combined. Stir in the chopped nuts, distributing them evenly throughout the dough. Divide the dough into 4 pieces and wrap tightly. Keep the dough at room temperature. It will be fairly soft.

Put a piece of dough into the cookie press. Extrude it onto a baking sheet in 7-inch strips. Form heart shapes by overlapping the ends of each strip, making an "x" at the top of the heart, and shaping the sides as you work your way around. Finish the heart by pinching together the bottom point. Space the cookies 1 1/2 inches apart, and freeze them (see Tips for Baking & Decorating, page 14).

Bake the cookies until they are lightly browned, 8 to 10 minutes. Carefully transfer the cookies to wire racks and let them cool. Continue shaping and baking the cookies until all the dough is used. Dust the cookies with confectioners' sugar while they are still slightly warm. *Makes 36 cookies*

Chocolate Peanut Butter Lollipops

For the inner child in us all—a chocolate chip cookie eaten like a lollipop.
Rolled oats and peanut butter add crunch to these chewy cookies. Pot them in painted clay, add greenery and
dyed eggs for a grown-up Easter basket.

1 1/2 cup flour
1 teaspoon baking powder
1/2 cup unsalted butter, at room temperature
3/4 cup granulated sugar
3/4 cup firmly packed light brown sugar
2 large eggs, at room temperature, lightly beaten
1 teaspoon vanilla extract
1/2 cup chunky peanut butter
1 1/2 cups rolled oats
2 cups semisweet chocolate chips

12 (8-inch long) lollipop sticks

Heat the oven to 325°. Brush a heart-shaped lollipop cookie mold with butter. In a mixing bowl, whisk together the flour and baking powder, and set aside.

Cream the butter and sugars with an electric mixer set on medium speed until light and fluffy. Beat in the eggs and vanilla extract. On low speed, gradually beat in the flour mixture until well combined. Stir in the peanut butter, rolled oats, and chocolate chips.

Spoon the dough into the cookie molds, filling them just to the top. Insert the lollipop sticks 2 inches into the dough. Bake the cookies until lightly browned, 10 to 12 minutes. Let the cookies cool in the molds for 5 minutes, then transfer them to wire racks and let cool completely. Continue shaping and baking the cookies until all the dough is used. *Makes 12 cookies*

Note: Lollipop cookie molds and sticks are available at bakery supply shops.

Cakes & Tarts

MEYER LEMON POUND CAKE

ROYAL HEARTS CUPCAKES

COCONUT CONFETTI CUPCAKES

VERY BERRY TART

RHUBARB & STRAWBERRY COUNTRY TART

MANDARIN ORANGE ANGEL CAKE

FOURTH OF JULY FINALE

CHOCOLATE AMARETTO TORTE

LEMON MERINGUE TART WITH

BLUEBERRY COMPOTE

Meyer Lemon Pound Cake

This is a beautifully simple, sugar-dusted cake, decorated without frosting in the European tradition. For a special birthday, bake the cake in a heart-shaped mold, and decorate it with sugared edible flowers and French wax candles.

2 cups cake flour
1/2 teaspoon cream of tartar
1/4 teaspoon baking soda
1/4 teaspoon salt
1 cup unsalted butter, at room temperature
1 1/2 cups granulated sugar
5 large eggs, at room temperature
1 teaspoon vanilla extract

1 tablespoon finely grated lemon zest
Confectioners' sugar, for dusting

MEYER LEMON SYRUP
1/2 cup freshly squeezed Meyer lemon juice
1/2 cup steeped herbal lemon tea
1 cup granulated sugar

Heat the oven to 325°. Brush a 6-cup heart-shaped cake pan with butter, and dust it with flour. Sift together the flour, cream of tartar, baking soda, and salt, and set aside.

Cream the butter and granulated sugar with an electric mixer set on medium speed until light and fluffy. Beat in the eggs, one at a time, beating well after each addition. Beat in the vanilla extract and lemon zest. On low speed, gradually beat in the dry ingredients just until the batter is evenly mixed. The batter will be stiff. Pour the batter into the pan and bake until a toothpick inserted in the center of the cake comes out clean, 40 to 50 minutes.

In the meantime, make the syrup. Combine the lemon juice, tea, and sugar in a small saucepan, bring to a boil, and cook until the syrup thickens, about 5 minutes. Remove the pan from the heat and let the syrup cool.

Let the cake cool in the pan 10 minutes. Pierce the flat side of the cake all over with a toothpick to help it absorb the syrup, and slowly pour the syrup over the cake and down the sides. Let the cake cool in the pan 10 minutes more. Transfer the cake to a wire rack and let it cool completely. Dust the cake with confectioners' sugar and serve. *Serves 12*

Note: The Meyer lemon is a lemon in name only. It is a citrus fruit, with juice that is less acidic than conventional lemons and flesh that is pinkish in color. Look for the Meyer lemon in produce markets from December to May. If Meyer lemons are out of season, substitute an equal amount of regular lemon juice. This cake can also be made in a 6-cup Bundt pan.

Royal Hearts Cupcakes

What would a tea party or afternoon game of bridge be without these chocolate and peppermint flavored cakes?
The fluffiest of pink frostings and crushed peppermint candies decorate these royal treats.

1¹/2 cups cake flour

1¹/2 cups granulated sugar

1 teaspoon baking soda

¹/4 teaspoon baking powder

¹/2 teaspoon salt

¹/2 cup unsweetened cocoa

1 cup warm water

2 large eggs, at room temperature

¹/2 cup vegetable oil

1 teaspoon vanilla extract

³/4 cup mint chocolate chips

4 ounces peppermint candies, crushed

FLUFFY PINK FROSTING

1¹/2 cups granulated sugar

¹/4 cup water

2 large egg whites

1 teaspoon light corn syrup

¹/4 teaspoon salt

1 teaspoon peppermint extract

2 drops red food coloring

Heat the oven to 350°. Line a standard cupcake tin with paper cupcake cups. In a mixing bowl, whisk together the cake flour, sugar, baking soda, baking powder, and salt, and set aside.

Dissolve the cocoa in the warm water. Beat in the eggs, oil, and vanilla extract by hand until well combined. Gradually beat in the dry ingredients just until the batter is evenly mixed. Fold in the mint chocolate chips.

Spoon the batter into the cupcake cups, filling them three-quarters full. Bake the cupcakes until a toothpick inserted in the center comes out clean, 25 to 30 minutes. Transfer the cupcakes to wire racks and let them cool completely.

To make the Fluffy Pink Frosting: In a double boiler, combine the sugar, water, egg whites, corn syrup, and salt over low heat. Carefully beat the mixture with a handheld electric mixer set on medium speed until stiff peaks form, about 7 minutes. Remove the mixture from the heat and stir in the peppermint extract and red food coloring, blending well to distribute the color. Let the frosting cool completely.

When the cupcakes and frosting are cool, frost the cupcakes with Fluffy Pink Frosting and sprinkle with the crushed peppermint candies. *Makes 12 cupcakes*

Coconut Confetti Cupcakes

For a hands-on approach to a child's birthday party, let the kids dye the coconut—the brighter, the better—and decorate the tops of these cupcakes with small trinkets or toys.

1¹/2 cups cake flour
¹/2 teaspoon baking soda
¹/2 teaspoon salt
¹/2 cup unsalted butter, at room temperature
1 cup granulated sugar
2 large eggs, at room temperature
1 teaspoon vanilla extract
¹/2 cup buttermilk
4 cups shredded sweetened coconut
Assorted food colorings

BUTTERCREAM FROSTING
³/4 cup unsalted butter, at room temperature
4 cups confectioners' sugar
2 teaspoons vanilla extract
4 to 6 teaspoons milk

Heat the oven to 350°. Line a standard cupcake tin with paper cupcake cups. Sift together the cake flour, baking soda, and salt, and set aside.

Cream the butter and sugar with an electric mixer set on medium speed until light and fluffy. Beat in the eggs, one at a time, beating well after each addition. Beat in the vanilla extract. On low speed, gradually beat the dry ingredients, alternating with the buttermilk, in two batches, just until the batter is evenly mixed.

Spoon the batter into the cupcake cups, filling them three-quarters full. Bake the cupcakes until a toothpick inserted in the center comes out clean, 25 to 30 minutes. Transfer the cupcakes to wire racks and let them cool completely.

In the meantime, prepare the coconut. For each color you would like to make, measure 1 cup coconut, and put it in a half-gallon plastic bag or glass jar. Add food coloring, one drop at a time, seal the bag or jar, and shake until the coconut is colored to your liking. The more food coloring you add, the brighter the coconut will be.

To make the Buttercream Frosting: Cream the butter and sugar with an electric mixture set on medium speed until light and fluffy. Beat in vanilla extract. On low speed, gradually beat in enough milk to yield a good spreading consistency.

When the cupcakes are cool, frost them with Buttercream Frosting and sprinkle with colored coconut. *Makes 12 cupcakes*

Very Berry Tart

Here, a chocolate crumb crust holds a sweetened ricotta filling that is topped with fresh seasonal berries and drizzled with honey. This tart is quick and easy to make, and company will love it.

COOKIE CRUST

2 cups crushed chocolate wafers

¹/₄ cup sugar

¹/₈ teaspoon salt

2 tablespoons unsalted butter, melted and cooled

1 large egg white, at room temperature, lightly beaten

FILLING

2 pounds low-fat ricotta, well drained

2 tablespoons plus ¹/₄ cup orange blossom honey

1 tablespoon finely grated orange zest

1 teaspoon vanilla extract

1 pint strawberries, rinsed, hulled, and well drained

1 pint raspberries, rinsed and well drained

¹/₂ pint blueberries, rinsed and well drained

¹/₂ pint blackberries, rinsed and well drained

Heat the oven to 350°. Brush a 10-inch loose-bottomed heart-shaped tart pan with butter.

To make the cookie crust: Combine the crushed chocolate wafers, sugar, and salt. Add the melted butter and egg white, and stir until the mixture comes together. With the palm of your hand, press the mixture into the tart pan, making sure the joint between the pan bottom and side is well covered. Bake the crust until dry, 15 to 20 minutes. Transfer the crust to a wire rack and let it cool completely.

In the meantime, make the filling. Beat the drained ricotta, 2 tablespoons honey, orange zest, and vanilla extract with an electric mixer set on a low speed until smooth. Chill this mixture for 30 minutes.

Fill the cooled crust with the ricotta mixture and refrigerate 1 hour. To serve, place the berries on top of the tart in a decorative pattern and drizzle with the remaining honey.

Serves 6 to 8

Rhubarb & Strawberry Country Tart

A cross between a tart and custard, this classic combination of rhubarb and strawberry in tender pastry is best served in a shallow bowl—the perfect end to a Sunday brunch. Feel free to pour a little heavy cream on top.

PASTRY
1¼ cups flour
1 tablespoon granulated sugar
⅛ teaspoon salt
½ cup unsalted butter, chilled
1 large egg, at room temperature

FILLING
1½ cups granulated sugar
4 tablespoons flour
⅛ teaspoon salt
2 large eggs, at room temperature, beaten
3 cups rhubarb, cut into ½-inch pieces
1½ cups strawberries, rinsed, well drained, and cut into quarters
1 large egg yolk, at room temperature, beaten with 1 tablespoon water

To make the pastry: Sift together the flour, sugar, and salt. Cut the chilled butter into the dry ingredients with a pastry blender until the mixture resembles coarse meal. Add the egg and mix quickly by hand until the dough comes together to form a loose ball. Flatten the dough into a disk, wrap tightly, and refrigerate until firm, about 2 hours.

On a lightly floured board, roll the dough to an ⅛-inch thickness. Using a pan lid as your guide, cut out a round of dough 12 inches in diameter. Line a 9-inch pie plate with the dough. Do not trim the dough even with the top of the plate. Refrigerate the tart shell until firm, about 15 minutes. Heat the oven to 450°.

To make the filling: Sift together the sugar, flour, and salt. Add the eggs, beating until the batter is smooth. Stir in the rhubarb and strawberries and pour the filling into the pie shell. Fold the edge of the dough over the filling to form a loose ruffle. Brush the dough with the egg-water wash.

Bake the tart at 450° for 10 minutes. Reduce the heat to 350°, and continue baking until the pastry is lightly browned and the filling is set, about 30 minutes more. Transfer the tart to a wire rack and let it cool slightly. Serve warm. *Serves 6*

Mandarin Orange Angel Cake

Made with mandarin oranges, this cake is delicious on its own, and even better iced with a chocolate glaze. Candied orange peel decorates the top. This cake makes a lovely addition to the menu for a baby shower.

1 cup cake flour
1 1/2 cups large egg whites (about 12), at room temperature
1 1/2 cups granulated sugar
1 teaspoon cream of tartar
3 tablespoons freshly squeezed mandarin orange juice
2 tablespoons finely grated mandarin orange peel
1 recipe Chocolate Glaze (pages 59–60)

CANDIED ORANGE PEEL

2 mandarin oranges
1/2 cup granulated sugar
1/4 cup water

Heat the oven to 350°. Sift the flour.

Beat the egg whites with an electric mixer set on medium speed just until broken up, about 1 minute. Gradually beat in the sugar and cream of tartar while slowly increasing mixing speed. Beat the mixture on high speed just until stiff peaks form. The egg whites will be stiff and glossy, but should not be dry. Beat in the mandarin orange juice.

With a rubber spatula, gently fold the sifted flour into the egg whites just until incorporated. Fold in the orange peel. Spoon the batter into a 10-inch, ungreased, loose-bottomed tube pan, taking care to fully cover the bottom of the pan. Bake the cake until a toothpick inserted in the center comes out clean, 25 to 30 minutes. Let the cake cool 10 minutes, then invert the pan and hang it upside down until the cake is completely cool, about 1 hour.

In the meantime, make the candied orange peel. Using a sharp knife or vegetable peeler, cut 4-inch long strips of zest from the oranges. Stir together the sugar and water in a small saucepan. Cover the saucepan and bring the mixture to a boil. Reduce the heat, add the orange zest, cover, and simmer 10 minutes. Remove the pan from the heat and let the mixture cool. Stretch the zest on a wire rack to dry.

When the cake is cool, gently run a sharp, thin-bladed knife around the side and inner tube of the pan. Gently rap the pan on a counter to loosen the cake. Run the knife around the bottom of the pan and lift it from the cake. Put the cake on a wire rack. Slowly pour the Chocolate Glaze over the top of the cake, gently tilting the cake to distribute the glaze evenly and letting some drizzle decoratively down the side. Transfer the cake to a plate and arrange the candied orange peel on top. *Serves 8*

Note: If mandarins are not available, any sweet orange will do.

Fourth of July Finale

Trifle, classically made with fruit, tawny port, and nuts, is an English tradition. By using local summertime fruits and a sparkling candle on top, you can celebrate the Stars and Stripes with this sensational dessert.

MACERATED FRUIT

2 cups raspberries, rinsed and well drained

2 cups blueberries, rinsed and well drained,
or sliced purple plums

2 cups sliced white peaches or nectarines

3 tablespoons granulated sugar

6 tablespoons tawny port

CUSTARD

1 cup milk

1 cup light cream

7 large egg yolks, at room temperature, lightly beaten

1/4 cup granulated sugar

3 tablespoons flour

1 vanilla bean, split in half lengthwise

CAKE

1 cup cake flour

1/8 teaspoon salt

7 large eggs, at room temperature, separated

2/3 plus 1/3 cup granulated sugar

Finely grated zest and juice of 1 lemon

1/3 cup water

1 teaspoon vanilla extract

1/2 teaspoon cream of tartar

2 tablespoons tawny port

Amaretti cookies, crushed, for dusting

CHANTILLY CREAM

1 cup heavy cream

1/2 teaspoon vanilla extract

2 tablespoons sifted confectioners' sugar

To make the macerated fruit: Put the raspberries, blueberries, and peaches in separate bowls. Add 1 tablespoon granulated sugar and 2 tablespoons port to the fruit in each bowl, mix, and let them sit to blend their flavors, at least 1 hour.

To make the custard: Scald the milk and the cream, remove the pan from the heat, and keep the mixture warm. Combine the egg yolks, sugar, flour, and vanilla bean over medium heat in a heavy-based, nonreactive saucepan. Stir constantly with a wooden spoon until the mixture is smooth, light in color, and the sugar dissolves completely, about 5 minutes. Pour the scalded milk mixture into the egg yolk mixture and continue stirring until the custard thickens and coats the back of a spoon, about 10 minutes. Remove the pan from the heat and immediately transfer the custard into a clean bowl. Remove the vanilla bean from the bowl, scraping the seeds from the bean into the custard. Stir the custard occasionally and let it cool completely.

To make the cake: Heat the oven to 325°. Line the bottom of a 9-inch springform pan with parchment paper. Sift together the flour and the salt, and set aside. Beat the egg yolks and 2/3 cup granulated sugar with an electric mixer set on medium speed until pale and thick. Beat in the lemon zest and juice, water, and vanilla extract.

Beat the egg whites with an electric mixer set on medium speed just until broken up, about 1 minute. Gradually beat in 1/3 cup sugar and cream of tartar while slowly increasing the mixing speed. Beat the mixture on high speed just until stiff peaks form. The egg whites will be stiff and glossy, but should not be dry.

With a rubber spatula, gently fold the egg whites into the batter, being careful not to deflate them. Fold in the dry ingredients just until the flour disappears. Spoon the batter into the pan, making sure to completely cover the bottom and touch the sides, and bake until a toothpick inserted in the center of the cake comes out clean, 45 to 55 minutes. Let the cake cool in the pan 10 minutes. Run a thin-bladed knife around the side of the cake, spring open the pan, transfer the cake to a wire rack, and let it cool completely.

To assemble the trifle: With a serrated knife, cut the cake into three even layers. Drain the macerated fruit, reserving 3 tablespoons of each fruit's juice. Place the bottom layer of cake, bottom side down, in a glass trifle bowl. Sprinkle the cake layer with the reserved blueberry juice, spread the blueberries on top, and top with about 3/4 cup custard. Repeat this procedure, layering cake, juice, fruit, and custard, making the middle layer with the peaches and the top layer with the raspberries and remaining 2 tablespoons tawny port. Chill the trifle at least 1 hour before serving.

To make the Chantilly Cream: Beat the heavy cream with an electric mixer set on medium speed until it starts to thicken. Beat in the vanilla extract and confectioners' sugar until stiff peaks form. Refrigerate the cream until ready to use.

Just before serving, using a pastry bag fitted with a star tube, pipe rosettes of Chantilly cream on top of the trifle, or make a decorative swirl pattern of cream with a small spatula or the back of a spoon. Dust the trifle with crushed amaretti cookies and serve. *Serves 10 to 12*

Chocolate Amaretto Torte

In the ultimate chocolate indulgence, amaretto spikes a dense chocolate cake enveloped in a bittersweet chocolate glaze.
For the true romantic, serve with strawberries dipped in chocolate—perfect for an anniversary.

1/4 cup flour
1/2 cup ground toasted almonds
6 ounces bittersweet chocolate
3/4 cup unsalted butter, at room temperature
4 large eggs, at room temperature, separated
1/2 plus 1/4 cup granulated sugar
1 tablespoon amaretto
1/8 teaspoon cream of tartar
Unsweetened cocoa, for dusting

CHOCOLATE GLAZE
6 ounces bittersweet chocolate, cut into small chunks
4 tablespoons unsalted butter, at room temperature
1 tablespoon light corn syrup
1 tablespoon vegetable oil

8 strawberries, unhulled, rinsed and well drained

Heat the oven to 350°. Line the bottom of an 8-inch springform pan with parchment paper. Sift together the flour and ground nuts, and set aside. In a double boiler, melt the chocolate and butter over low heat, stirring frequently until smooth. Remove from the pan heat and let the mixture cool.

Beat the egg yolks and 1/2 cup sugar with an electric mixer set on medium speed until pale and thick. Beat in the amaretto. On low speed, gradually beat in the chocolate mixture, then the dry ingredients, just until the batter is evenly mixed, and set aside.

Beat the egg whites with an electric mixer set on medium speed just until broken up, about 1 minute. Gradually beat in the remaining 1/4 cup sugar and cream of tartar while slowly increasing the mixing speed. Beat the mixture on high speed just until stiff peaks form. The egg whites will be stiff and glossy, but should not be dry. *(continued on next page)*

With a rubber spatula, gently fold the egg whites into the batter, being careful not to deflate them. Pour the batter into the pan, smoothing the top with the spatula. Bake the cake until a toothpick inserted in the center comes out clean, 45 to 50 minutes. Let the cake cool in the pan 5 minutes. Unmold the cake onto an 8-inch cardboard cake round. Transfer the cake on the cardboard round to a wire rack and let it cool completely.

To make the Chocolate Glaze: In a double boiler, melt the chocolate and butter over low heat, stirring frequently until smooth. Remove the mixture from the heat and stir in the corn syrup and oil. For smoothness, strain the glaze through a fine-meshed sieve into a glass measuring cup. Set aside 1/3 cup glaze for the strawberries.

To make the chocolate-dipped strawberries: Dip the strawberries in the reserved Chocolate Glaze, covering them halfway, set them on waxed paper, and let them sit until the glaze is set.

When the cake is cool, pour over the Chocolate Glaze. Working quickly, pour the glaze over the cake, gently tilting the cake to distribute the glaze evenly. Return the cake to the wire rack until the glaze is completely set, about 1 hour. Place a doily on top of the cake, dust with cocoa and remove the doily. Serve with the chocolate-dipped strawberries. *Serves 8*

Note: Eight-inch cardboard cake rounds and doilies are available at bakery supply shops.

Lemon Meringue Tart with Blueberry Compote

A summertime barbecue favorite, this rich pastry is filled with lemon curd and topped with meringue. Sweet blueberry compote is a beautiful and flavorful complement to the tart lemon.

PASTRY

1 cup unsalted butter, chilled
2 cups flour
$1/4$ teaspoon salt
$1/2$ cup cold water

FILLING

3 large eggs, at room temperature, separated
$1/4$ plus $1/2$ cup granulated sugar
Finely grated zest and freshly squeezed juice of 1 large lemon
1 tablespoon unsalted butter, at room temperature
$1/8$ teaspoon cream of tartar

BLUEBERRY COMPOTE

3 cups blueberries, rinsed and well drained
$1/4$ cup granulated sugar

To make the pastry: Cut the butter into 1-inch pieces. In the bowl of a food processor, with the metal blade attached, pulse the butter, flour, and salt until pea-sized pieces form. Slowly pour the cold water through the feed tube, and continue processing until the dough comes together to form a loose ball. Flatten the dough into a disk, wrap tightly, and refrigerate until firm, about 1 hour.

To make the lemon curd filling: Cook the egg yolks, lemon juice, and $1/4$ cup of the sugar in a nonreactive saucepan over low heat until the mixture has thickened and coats the back of a spoon, about 10 minutes. Remove the pan from the heat, stir in the butter until it melts, and refrigerate until cool.

On a lightly floured board, roll the dough to an $1/8$-inch thickness. Using a pan lid as your guide, cut out a round of dough 11 inches in diameter. Line a 9-inch loose-bottomed tart pan with the dough and trim the top edge of the dough

62

even with the top of the pan. Prick the tart shell with the tines of a fork and refrigerate until firm, about 15 minutes. Heat the oven to 400°.

Cover the tart shell with a piece of parchment paper and fill with dried beans or rice. Bake the tart shell 10 minutes, reduce the heat to 350°, and continue baking until the pastry is lightly browned, about 10 minutes more. Transfer the tart shell to a wire rack, carefully remove the parchment paper and beans, and let it cool completely. Reduce the heat to 300°.

When the tart shell is completely cool, beat the egg whites with an electric mixer set on low speed until broken up, about 1 minute. Gradually beat in the remaining $1/2$ cup sugar and cream of tartar while slowly increasing mixing speed. Beat on high speed just until stiff peaks form. The egg whites will be stiff and glossy, but should not be dry.

Pour the lemon curd into the tart shell, filling it three-quarters full. With a small spatula or the back of a spoon, spread the egg whites over top of the lemon curd, making sure they touch the side of the shell. Bake the tart until lightly browned, about 3 minutes. Transfer the tart to a wire rack and let it cool completely.

To make the Blueberry Compote: Cook the blueberries and sugar in a saucepan over medium heat until the berries begin to release their juice, about 10 minutes. Remove the pan from the heat, and let the compote cool to room temperature. Serve the tart with the blueberry compote. *Serves 6 to 8*

Quick Breads & Pastries

JEWELED SCONES

APPLE BLUEBERRY TURNOVERS

PEACH-POCKET CORNMEAL MUFFINS

CHERRY & MARZIPAN STRUDEL

CHOCOLATE BANANA MUFFINS

TROPICAL TEA CAKE WITH RUM GLAZE

MARBLED MOCHA PECAN COFFEECAKE

Jeweled Scones

The "jewels" in these scones are colorful dried fruits and pistachios, with a sprinkling of decorative sugar on top—
sure to be best-sellers at the bake sale.

1¹/4 cups flour
³/4 cup whole wheat flour
4 tablespoons granulated sugar
1 tablespoon baking powder
¹/4 teaspoon salt
¹/2 cup unsalted butter, chilled
1 large egg, at room temperature
¹/2 cup buttermilk
¹/2 cup dried cranberries
¹/2 cup chopped dried apricots
¹/4 cup chopped pistachios
1 teaspoon finely grated orange zest
2 tablespoons decorative sugar (optional)

Heat the oven to 375°. Brush a heart-shaped scone pan with butter. In a mixing bowl, whisk together the flours, sugar, baking powder, and salt. Cut the chilled butter into the dry ingredients with a pastry blender until the mixture resembles coarse meal, and make a well in the center. Combine the egg and buttermilk, and pour into the well. Stir just until the dry ingredients are moistened. Gently fold in the cranberries, apricots, pistachios, and orange zest. Do not overmix.

Spoon the batter into the pan, sprinkle with decorative sugar, and bake until lightly browned, 15 to 20 minutes. Transfer the scones to a wire rack and let them cool slightly. Serve warm. *Makes 6 scones*

Note: To shape the scones by hand, on a lightly floured board, pat the dough into an 8-inch disk. Cut the dough into 6 wedges, sprinkle with decorative sugar, and bake as directed.

Apple Blueberry Turnovers

Freshly baked turnovers and fresh-cut flowers are the perfect way to acknowledge the kindness of a friend.

PASTRY

1 cup unsalted butter, chilled
2 cups flour
1/4 teaspoon salt
1/2 cup water, chilled

FILLING

8 Granny Smith or pippin apples
3 tablespoons granulated sugar
2 tablespoons unsalted butter, at room temperature
1 tablespoon Calvados or applejack
1 cup blueberries, rinsed and well drained
1 large egg, at room temperature, lightly beaten
1 tablespoon milk
1/4 cup apple jelly, stirred

To make the pastry: Cut the butter into 1-inch pieces. In the bowl of a food processor, with the metal blade attached, pulse the butter, flour, and salt until pea-sized pieces form. Slowly pour the water through the feed tube, and continue pulsing until the dough comes together to form a loose ball. Flatten the ball into a disk, wrap tightly, and refrigerate until firm, about 1 hour.

In the meantime, make the filling. Peel, core, and coarsely chop the apples. Cook the apples, sugar, and butter in a saucepan over low heat just until tender, about 20 minutes. Remove the pan from the heat and let the mixture cool. Stir in the Calvados and blueberries, and set aside.

Line a baking sheet with parchment paper. On a lightly floured board, roll the dough to an 1/8-inch thickness. With a pastry wheel, cut 8 (6-inch) rounds, and transfer them to the baking sheet. Spoon 1/3 cup filling into the center of each round. Fold the rounds in half, forming half-moon shapes, and gently press the edges together. Mix together the egg and milk, and brush it onto the tops of the turnovers. Refrigerate the turnovers 10 minutes. Heat the oven to 400°.

Bake the turnovers 10 minutes. Reduce the heat to 350°, and continue baking until the turnovers are lightly browned, 20 to 30 minutes more. Remove the turnovers from the oven, and brush with the apple jelly. Transfer the turnovers to a wire rack and let them cool slightly. Serve warm. *Makes 8 turnovers*

Note: Thawed and well-drained frozen blueberries can be used when fresh berries are not in season.

Peach-Pocket Cornmeal Muffins

A touch of maple syrup makes these muffins moist and delicious. Kids love the surprise pocket of peach preserves inside.
Make them on a lazy Sunday morning when it's chilly outside.

1 cup flour
1 cup cornmeal
1 tablespoon granulated sugar
1 tablespoon baking powder
$1/4$ teaspoon salt

$2/3$ cup milk
$1/4$ cup unsalted butter, melted and cooled
1 large egg, at room temperature
$1/3$ cup maple syrup
$1/2$ cup peach preserves

Heat the oven to 400°. Line a standard muffin tin with 8 paper muffin cups. Sift together the flour, cornmeal, granulated sugar, baking powder, and salt, and make a well in the center. Combine the milk, melted butter, egg, and maple syrup, and pour into the well. Stir just until the dry ingredients are moistened. Do not overmix.

Spoon 1 tablespoon of batter into each muffin cup, making a pocket in the batter with the back of a spoon. Spoon about 2 teaspoons peach preserves into each pocket, and cover with the remaining batter, stopping $1/2$ inch from the top. Bake the muffins until golden brown, 18 to 20 minutes. Transfer the muffins to a wire rack and let them cool slightly. Serve warm.
Makes 8 muffins

Cherry & Marzipan Strudel

Packaged phyllo works beautifully here. For richer flavor, I like to use a combination of marzipan and bread crumbs instead of the traditional chopped nuts. This strudel is a very nice addition to the holiday table.

4 tablespoons unsalted butter, at room temperature
3/4 cup bread crumbs
1/3 cup crumbled marzipan
2 cups cherries, rinsed, pitted, and well drained
1/2 cup golden raisins
2 teaspoons finely grated lemon zest

PASTRY
6 (18 x 14-inch) sheets phyllo dough
1/2 cup unsalted butter, melted
1/2 cup bread crumbs

Heat the oven to 375°. Line a baking sheet with parchment paper.

Heat the butter in a nonstick skillet over medium heat. Stir in the bread crumbs, and cook just until golden brown. Remove the pan from the heat, transfer the bread crumbs to a bowl, and let them cool. Cut the marzipan into the bread crumbs with a pastry blender until the mixture resembles coarse meal, and set aside.

To prepare the pastry: Cut each sheet of phyllo in half, making 12 (14 x 9-inch) sheets. Lay a sheet of phyllo on the baking sheet, covering remaining sheets with a damp towel and plastic wrap. Brush the sheet with 2 teaspoons melted butter and sprinkle with 2 teaspoons bread crumbs. Continue this procedure, stacking the sheets one on top of the other, until all the phyllo, butter, and bread crumbs are used.

Spread the cherries and raisins along a long side of the top sheet of phyllo. Sprinkle the marzipan mixture and lemon zest on top. Starting at the long side closest to the filling, roll up the strudel jelly-roll fashion, ending with it seam side down. Crimp the ends together and brush the top with butter. Bake the strudel until golden brown, 15 to 20 minutes. Let the strudel cool 10 minutes, cut it into slices with a serrated knife, and serve warm. *Makes 12 slices*

Note: Thawed and well-drained frozen cherries, or well-drained canned, can be used when fresh cherries are not in season.

Chocolate Banana Muffins

This recipe is based on one of my childhood favorites—a vanilla ice-cream sundae, with chocolate syrup, bananas, and salted peanuts. The sweet and salty combination is satisfying and unexpected. To dress up the muffins for gift giving, simply tie ribbons around the parchment paper cups.

2 cups flour
^{1}/$_2$ cup Dutch-process cocoa
1^1/$_2$ teaspoons baking powder
^{1}/$_4$ teaspoon salt
^{1}/$_2$ cup unsalted butter, at room temperature
1 cup granulated sugar
2 large eggs, at room temperature
2 teaspoons vanilla extract
2 cups mashed ripe bananas (about 5)
^{3}/$_4$ cup chopped, lightly salted peanuts

Heat the oven to 400°. Cut 12 (6-inch square) pieces of parchment paper. Place a square in each cup of a standard muffin tin, pushing down and spreading it to fill. In a mixing bowl, whisk together the flour, cocoa, baking powder, and salt, and set aside.

Cream the butter and sugar with an electric mixer set on medium speed until light and fluffy. Beat in the eggs and vanilla extract. By hand, stir in the mashed bananas, then the dry ingredients, just until the batter is evenly mixed. Spoon the batter into the muffin cups, filling them three-quarters full.

Bake the muffins 12 minutes. Add the chopped peanuts to the top of the muffins, and continue baking until a toothpick inserted in the center of a muffin comes out clean, about 8 minutes more. Transfer the muffins to a wire rack and let them cool slightly. Serve warm. *Makes 12 muffins*

Tropical Tea Cake with Rum Glaze

Serve this warmly spiced cake when it's cold outside. Fresh and dried papaya doubles the fruit flavor, and coconut and macadamia nuts add crunch.

2 cups flour
1 teaspoon baking powder
1/2 teaspoon baking soda
1 teaspoon ground cinnamon
1/2 teaspoon ground allspice
1/4 teaspoon ground nutmeg
1/4 teaspoon ground cloves
1/4 teaspoon salt
1/2 cup unsalted butter, at room temperature
1 cup firmly packed light brown sugar
2 large eggs, at room temperature
1 teaspoon vanilla extract

1 very ripe papaya, puréed
1 ripe banana, mashed
1 cup shredded, sweetened coconut
1 cup diced dried papaya
1/2 cup roasted and salted macadamia nuts,
coarsely chopped
Finely grated zest of 1 lime

RUM GLAZE

3 tablespoons rum
2 tablespoons unsalted butter, at room temperature
1 cup sifted confectioners' sugar

Heat the oven to 350°. Brush a 9 x 5-inch loaf pan with butter. Whisk together the flour, baking powder, baking soda, spices, and salt, and set aside.

Cream the butter and sugar with an electric mixer set on medium speed until light and fluffy. Beat in the eggs and vanilla extract. On low speed, beat in the puréed papaya and mashed banana. Gradually beat in the dry ingredients just until the batter is evenly mixed. Fold in the coconut, dried papaya, nuts, and lime zest, distributing them evenly throughout the batter. Pour the batter into the pan and bake until a toothpick inserted in the center comes out clean, about 1 hour.

In the meantime, make the glaze. Combine the rum and butter over medium heat in a small, heavy-based saucepan. Add the confectioners' sugar and stir until it dissolves completely. Remove the pan from the heat and keep the glaze slightly warm.

Let the cake cool in the pan 10 minutes. Transfer the cake to a wire rack and let it cool completely. Pour the glaze over the cake, and let the cake sit until the glaze is set. *Serves 8*

Note: This cake can be made the day before serving. Wrap it tightly in aluminum foil and keep it at room temperature. Glaze the cake shortly before you are ready to serve.

Marbled Mocha Pecan Coffeecake

In honor of the kaffeeklatsch tradition, share a slice of this cocoa and pecan-studded cake, and a cup of coffee, with a friend.

1¹/4 cups cake flour
1¹/2 teaspoon baking powder
¹/2 teaspoon baking soda
¹/4 teaspoon salt
¹/2 cup chopped pecans
¹/2 cup unsalted butter, at room temperature
³/4 cup plus 2 tablespoons granulated sugar
2 large eggs, at room temperature
¹/2 cup sour cream
1 teaspoon vanilla extract
1 tablespoon unsweetened cocoa
1 teaspoon instant espresso coffee
3 tablespoons water
1 cup confectioners' sugar

Heat the oven to 350°. Brush an 8-inch square baking pan with butter and dust it with flour. Sift together the flour, baking powder, baking soda, and salt, and set aside. Spread the nuts on a baking sheet and toast in the oven until fragrant, about 10 minutes. Let the nuts cool.

Cream the butter and ³/4 cup granulated sugar with an electric mixer set on medium speed until light and fluffy. Beat in the eggs, sour cream, and vanilla extract. On low speed, gradually beat in the dry ingredients just until the batter is evenly mixed. Stir in the chopped pecans. Pour the batter into the baking pan.

Sift together the remaining 2 tablespoons granulated sugar and the cocoa, and sprinkle the mixture over the batter. With a knife, cut through the batter, swirling the cocoa mixture to make a marbled effect.

Bake the cake until a toothpick inserted in the center comes out clean, 25 to 30 minutes. In the meantime, dissolve the instant coffee in the water, stir in the confectioners' sugar, and set aside. When the cake is done, drizzle the coffee mixture over top. Transfer the cake to a wire rack and let it cool slightly. Serve warm. *Serves 6 to 8*

Eggs & Batters

EYES OF THE BEHOLDER

FATHER'S DAY FRITTATA

POPPY SEED PANCAKES

CHALLAH FRENCH TOAST WITH PEAR APPLESAUCE

MEXICAN CHOCOLATE & RASPBERRY WAFFLES

CHOCOLATE CHIP BLINTZES WITH STRAWBERRIES

CORNCAKES WITH TOMATO-ORANGE SALSA

SMOKED TROUT & OAT CRISP CANAPÉS

ROASTED VEGETABLE PINWHEELS

POTATO CAKES WITH SHALLOTS & THYME

Eyes of the Beholder

After hunting Easter eggs in the garden, children will delight in finding one more in a heart-shaped nest.

4 large eggs, at room temperature
4 slices dense whole wheat bread
2 tablespoons unsalted butter, at room temperature
Salt and pepper to taste
1 small bunch of chives, cut into 1/2-inch pieces

Crack open each egg into a separate bowl, and set aside. With a 2-inch heart-shaped cookie cutter, cut a heart from the middle of each slice of bread. Heat 1/2 tablespoon butter in a large skillet over medium heat. Toast the heart-shaped cutouts in the skillet until golden brown on both sides. Remove them from the pan and keep warm.

Add more butter to the skillet and toast 2 slices of bread until golden brown. Flip the slices in the skillet and carefully pour an egg into each heart-shaped hole. Cover and cook until the eggs are done to your liking. Carefully remove the bread slices with eggs from the skillet with a spatula, cover, and keep warm. Repeat with the remaining butter, bread, and eggs. Season the eggs with salt and pepper, garnish with chives and toasted bread hearts, and serve. *Serves 4*

Father's Day Frittata

Whose dad wouldn't appreciate the hearty combination of crab, cheese, and Swiss chard? This frittata can be served straight from the oven, or at room temperature, making it perfect picnic fare.

8 ounces Swiss chard
2 tablespoons olive oil
1/2 cup chopped onion
1/4 cup chopped red bell pepper
1 tablespoon bread crumbs
3/4 cup crabmeat, flaked
1/2 cup grated Monterey jack cheese
1/2 cup grated Cheddar cheese
8 large eggs, at room temperature, beaten
Salt and pepper to taste
2 tablespoons grated Parmesan cheese

Heat the oven to 350°. Brush 4 (8-ounce) heart-shaped baking dishes or ramekins, or an 11 x 7-inch baking dish, with olive oil.

Remove and discard the tough stems from the chard, and blanch the leaves in boiling water. Drain the chard very well, chop it, and set aside. Heat the olive oil in a large skillet over medium-high heat. Sauté the onion and red bell pepper until soft, about 5 minutes. Add the chard and cook the mixture 2 minutes more. Transfer the vegetables to a large bowl, and let them cool.

Stir the bread crumbs, crabmeat, and jack and Cheddar cheeses into the vegetable mixture. Add the beaten eggs and stir until well combined. Season with salt and pepper. Pour the mixture into the baking dishes and sprinkle with Parmesan cheese. Bake the frittata until lightly browned, 15 to 20 minutes. *Serves 4*

Poppy Seed Pancakes

Serve these light and fluffy pancakes as the English do, with a squeeze of lemon and a dusting of confectioners' sugar.

1 cup flour
1 teaspoon baking powder
1/4 teaspoon baking soda
1/8 teaspoon salt
1 large egg, at room temperature
1/4 cup confectioners' sugar
1/4 cup unsalted butter, melted
3/4 cup milk
1 teaspoon vanilla extract
1 tablespoon poppy seeds
2 teaspoons finely grated lemon zest
1 lemon, cut into wedges
Confectioners' sugar, for dusting

In a mixing bowl, whisk together the flour, baking powder, baking soda, and salt, and set aside.

Beat the egg, confectioners' sugar, and melted butter until smooth. Stir in the dry ingredients, alternating with the milk, in two batches, just until the batter is evenly mixed. Gently stir in the vanilla extract, poppy seeds, and lemon zest.

Heat a skillet over medium-high heat and brush with butter. Drop the batter into the skillet by tablespoonfuls, and cook the pancakes until quite a few bubbles form on the surface. Flip the pancakes and continue cooking until the bottoms are golden brown. Remove the pancakes from skillet and keep them warm. Continue cooking the pancakes until all the batter is used. Serve them hot, with a squeeze of lemon juice and a dusting of confectioners' sugar. *Serves 4*

Challah French Toast with Pear Applesauce

Welcome everyone into the kitchen with this recipe the whole family can participate in making.
Let the youngest member stir in the cinnamon hearts.

PEAR APPLESAUCE

2 Granny Smith or pippin apples
1 pear
^{1}/4 cup water
2 tablespoons granulated sugar
1^1/2 teaspoons cinnamon candy hearts

FRENCH TOAST

4 large eggs, at room temperature
^{1}/2 cup milk
2 teaspoons granulated sugar
1 teaspoon vanilla extract
^{1}/4 teaspoon ground cinnamon
^{1}/8 teaspoon salt
8 slices challah bread
3 tablespoons unsalted butter, at room temperature
Confectioners' sugar, for dusting

To make the Pear Applesauce: Peel, core, and coarsely chop the apples and pear. Cook the fruit, water, and sugar in a saucepan over medium heat until the fruit is soft, 15 to 20 minutes. Remove the pan from the heat, and mash the fruit with a potato masher, leaving it a little chunky. Stir in the cinnamon hearts.

Whisk together the eggs, milk, granulated sugar, vanilla extract, cinnamon, and salt until well combined. Pour the egg mixture into a wide, shallow pan. Lay the challah slices in the egg mixture in a single layer, and let them sit, turning once, until all the egg is absorbed, 5 to 10 minutes.

Heat some of the butter in a large, nonstick skillet over medium heat. Cook the challah slices in batches until golden and crisp, about 2 minutes on each side. Serve warm with the Pear Applesauce and a dusting of confectioners' sugar. *Serves 4*

Mexican Chocolate & Raspberry Waffles

Here are three treats for Mom on her special day—breakfast in bed, chocolate-flavored waffles, and fresh berries.
A dollop of freshly whipped cream, if you like, makes an even four.

1 ounce unsweetened chocolate
1 ounce Mexican chocolate, grated
1¹/₂ cup cake flour
2 teaspoons baking powder
¹/₄ teaspoon salt
¹/₂ cup unsalted butter, at room temperature
1 cup granulated sugar
2 large eggs, at room temperature, beaten
1 teaspoon vanilla extract
¹/₂ cup milk
Confectioners' sugar, for dusting
1 pint raspberries, rinsed and well drained

In a double boiler, melt the unsweetened chocolate over low heat, stirring frequently until smooth. Remove from the heat, stir in the Mexican chocolate, and let cool. Sift together the flour, baking powder, and salt, and set aside. Heat the waffle iron.

Cream the butter and sugar with an electric mixer set on medium speed until light and fluffy. Beat in the eggs and vanilla extract, then beat in the chocolate mixture. On low speed, gradually beat in the dry ingredients, alternating with the milk, in two batches, just until the batter is evenly mixed.

Cook the waffle batter according to the manufacturer's directions. Dust the waffles with confectioners' sugar and serve with raspberries. *Serves 4*

Note: Mexican chocolate is a combination of cinnamon, sugar, and cocoa. It is available in bar form at Latin markets. Look for Ibarra and Abuelita brands. These waffles can be made in either a heart-shaped or round waffle iron.

Chocolate Chip Blintzes with Strawberries

This recipe was coaxed from my friend Andrea, the authority on Jewish cooking. Following tradition, these blintzes are made with curd cheese and fruit preserves. Chocolate chips and fresh strawberries are my own additions.

BLINTZE BATTER
3/4 cup flour
2 large eggs
1 cup milk
1/2 teaspoon salt

FILLING
15 ounces ricotta cheese
2 ounces cream cheese, at room temperature

1 large egg
1 tablespoon light cream
2 plus 1 tablespoons granulated sugar
1/4 teaspoon salt
1/3 cup mini chocolate chips
1 pint strawberries, rinsed, hulled, and well drained
1 tablespoon unsalted butter, melted
1/4 cup sour cream

To make the blintzes: Sift the flour. Combine the eggs, milk, flour, and salt with an electric mixer set on low speed. Heat a crepe pan over medium-high heat and brush with butter. Pour 1/4 cup batter into the pan, quickly tilting the pan to distribute the batter evenly. Cook until the bottom side of the blintze is lightly browned. Do not flip the blintze, but turn it out onto a damp dish towel, cooked side down. Continue cooking the blintzes, stacking them as you go, until all the batter is used.

To make the filling: Mix the cheeses, egg, light cream, 2 tablespoons sugar, and salt until well combined. Fold in the chocolate chips, and set aside. Slice the strawberries, mix with the remaining sugar, and set aside.

Heat the oven to 350°. Brush a baking sheet with butter. Spoon 2 tablespoons filling into the center of each blintze, cooked side up. Turn three sides of the blintze over the filling, and roll up. Place the blintzes, seam side down, on the baking sheet and brush them with melted butter. Bake for 15 minutes, turn the blintzes, and continue baking until all sides are lightly browned, 10 to 15 minutes more. Top with the sliced strawberries and a dollop of sour cream, and serve. *Serves 4*

Note: Blintzes can be made up to 2 hours ahead. Cover them lightly until you are ready to fill and bake. Or they can be made, filled, and held in the refrigerator several hours before baking.

Corncakes with Tomato-Orange Salsa

Ring in the new year with these salsa-topped, piquant pancakes and glasses of sparkling wine.

TOMATO-ORANGE SALSA
4 plum tomatoes, chopped
1 orange, peeled, segmented, and chopped
1/2 cup finely chopped red onion
1/2 cup chopped cilantro
1 teaspoon ground cumin
Salt and pepper to taste

CORNCAKES
1 1/4 cups cornmeal
1/4 cup flour
1 1/2 teaspoons baking powder
1/2 teaspoon crushed red pepper flakes
1/2 teaspoon salt
1/4 cup finely chopped green onions
3/4 cup milk
1 large egg, at room temperature, lightly beaten
1 tablespoon vegetable oil
Vegetable oil
1/2 cup sour cream

To make the Tomato-Orange Salsa: Combine the tomatoes, orange, red onion, cilantro, and cumin. Season with salt and pepper, and let sit before serving to blend the flavors, about 30 minutes.

To make the Corncakes: In a mixing bowl, whisk together the cornmeal, flour, baking powder, red pepper flakes, salt, and green onion, and make a well in the center. Combine the milk, egg, and 1 tablespoon vegetable oil, and pour into the well. Stir just until the dry ingredients are moistened. Do not overmix.

Heat some vegetable oil in a nonstick skillet. Drop the batter into the skillet by tablespoonfuls, and cook the corncakes until golden brown, about 2 minutes on each side. Transfer the corncakes to paper towels to drain, then top with sour cream and salsa, and serve. *Serves 4 to 6 as a first course*

Menu for a Baby Shower

ROASTED VEGETABLE PINWHEELS

SMOKED TROUT & OAT CRISP CANAPÉS

POTATO CAKES WITH SHALLOTS & THYME

MANDARIN ORANGE ANGEL CAKE

ICED PAPAYA MINT TEA

FRESHLY SQUEEZED LEMONADE

SPARKLING WINES

Smoked Trout & Oat Crisp Canapés

The unusual and delicious pairing of smoke-scented trout and chewy, crispy rolled oats makes these canapés a great addition to entertaining menus. The spread is best made ahead, allowing the flavors time to blend. The oat crisps can be made up to three days in advance, and stored in an airtight container.

1 pound cream cheese, at room temperature
4 ounces smoked trout, flaked
1/2 teaspoon horseradish
2 tablespoons minced red onion
Dash of freshly squeezed lemon juice
10 ounces frozen chopped spinach, thawed and well drained
Salt and pepper to taste
Finely cut strips of lemon zest, for garnish

OAT CRISPS
4 cups rolled oats
1 teaspoon paprika
1/2 teaspoon baking soda
1/2 teaspoon salt
1/4 cup unsalted butter, at room temperature
1 cup plus 2 tablespoons water

Beat the cream cheese with an electric mixer set on medium speed until smooth. Stir in the smoked trout, horseradish, onion, and lemon juice, and mix until well combined. Fold in the spinach, and season with salt and pepper. Refrigerate the mixture to blend the flavors, at least 2 hours or overnight.

To make the Oat Crisps: Heat the oven to 325°. Line a baking sheet with parchment paper. In a mixing bowl, whisk together the oats, paprika, baking soda, and salt, and set aside. Bring the butter and water to a boil in a small saucepan. Remove the pan from the heat, and add the mixture to the oat mixture. Mix together with your hands, and knead the dough into a loose ball.

Between 2 pieces of parchment paper, roll the dough to a 1/4-inch thickness. Cut the dough into 12 squares. Cut the squares in half, on the diagonal, into wedges, and transfer the shapes to the baking sheet. Bake the wedges until crisp and golden brown, about 45 minutes. Transfer the crisps to wire racks and let them cool completely.

Just before serving, spread crisps with the smoked trout mixture and garnish with strips of lemon zest. *Makes 24 canapés*

Roasted Vegetable Pinwheels

Here, I've used whole wheat, but spinach, tomato, or herb tortillas work equally well for these tasty vegetarian hors d'oeuvres.
The filling is best made ahead, allowing the flavors time to blend.

1 red bell pepper
1 yellow star burst or zucchini squash
1 small red onion
1 carrot
3 asparagus spears
1/4 cup olive oil

Salt and pepper to taste
1 pound cream cheese, at room temperature
6 (8-inch) whole wheat flour tortillas
4 teaspoons powdered egg whites
1/4 cup warm water
1 cup finely chopped fresh parsley

Heat the oven to 450°. Put the vegetables in a baking dish just big enough to hold them in one layer without crowding. Drizzle the olive oil on top and season with salt and pepper. Roast the vegetables until al dente, about 25 minutes. Let all the vegetables cool except for the bell pepper. Place it in a brown paper bag, seal the bag, and let the pepper steam 10 minutes. When it is cool enough to handle, peel away the skin under running water.

In the bowl of a food processor, with the metal blade attached, work the vegetables just until coarsely chopped. Transfer the vegetables to a fine mesh strainer, and drain well. Work the cream cheese in the food processor until smooth. Add the drained vegetables and pulse the mixture to yield a good spreading consistency. Adjust its seasoning and refrigerate the filling to blend the flavors, at least 2 hours or overnight.

To assemble the pinwheels: Spread about 1/4 cup vegetable mixture on each tortilla, leaving a 1/2-inch border all the way around. Roll up the tortillas, jelly-roll fashion, wrap each tightly, and refrigerate until they are firm enough to cut, about 2 hours. Just before serving, beat the powdered egg whites and water with an electric mixer set on low speed until all the water is absorbed, about 2 minutes. Brush the logs with the egg white mixture, roll in the finely chopped parsley, and cut into 1-inch slices. *Makes 36 slices*

Note: Powdered egg whites are available in baking supply shops or from catalogs (page 108).

Potato Cakes with Shallots & Thyme

Sweet roasted shallots and savory thyme elevate the simple mashed potato to worthy party fare.

4 large shallots
Olive oil
2 pounds Yukon gold potatoes, scrubbed
3 tablespoons unsalted butter, at room temperature

^{1}/2 cup milk
1 teaspoon dried thyme
Salt and pepper to taste
Fresh thyme sprigs

Heat the oven to 400°. Brush a small baking dish with oil. Cut off the stem end of each shallot. Put the shallots in the baking dish, drizzle them with olive oil, and roast until very soft, 20 to 30 minutes. When cool enough to handle, squeeze the shallots from their skins, chop them, and set aside.

In the meantime, put the potatoes in a large pot and cover them with cold water. Bring the water to a boil, cover the pot, and reduce the heat. Simmer the potatoes until tender, 20 to 30 minutes. Remove the pan from the heat and let the potatoes cool. Peel the potatoes and mash them. Add the chopped shallots, butter, milk, and dried thyme, and mix until well combined. Season with salt and pepper.

Line two baking sheets with aluminum foil, and brush the foil with olive oil. Spread the mashed potatoes evenly on a baking sheet to a ^{1}/2-inch thickness. Refrigerate the mixture until firm, about 2 hours.

With a 1^1/2-inch heart-shaped cookie cutter, cut out shapes from the chilled mashed potatoes. With a spatula, transfer the shapes to the other baking sheet. Brush the tops of the mashed potato hearts with olive oil and bake at 400° until lightly browned, 20 to 30 minutes. Serve warm, garnished with fresh thyme sprigs. *Makes 24 cakes*

ABOVE AND RIGHT:
Potato Cakes with Shallots & Thyme,
Roasted Vegetable Pinwheels,
and Smoked Trout & Oat Crisp Canapés
make a delightful menu for an afternoon
baby shower. Pierce linen napkins with
diaper pins to carry the theme through.

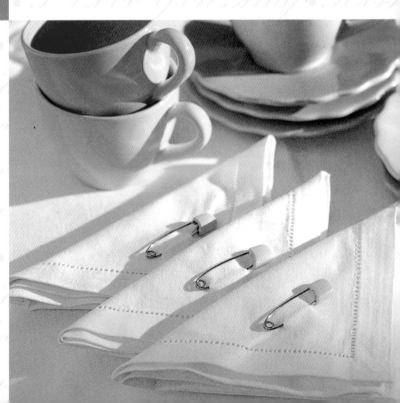

Baker's Notes

Record your favorite recipes, creative gift ideas, and special dates on the pages that follow.

_____

_____

_____

_____

_____

_____

_____

_____

_____

103

104

• I Love You • You're Mine • Be My Valentine •

You're My One and Only • I Love You Truly

• Kiss Me • I'm Yours Forever • Love & Kisses •

You're My One and Only • Love and Kisses

Metric Conversions

Liquid Weights

U.S. Measurements	Metric Equivalents
1/4 teaspoon	1.23 ml
1/2 teaspoon	2.5 ml
3/4 teaspoon	3.7 ml
1 teaspoon	5 ml
1 dessertspoon	10 ml
1 tablespoon (3 teaspoons)	15 ml
2 tablespoons (1 ounce)	30 ml
1/4 cup	60 ml
1/3 cup	80 ml
1/2 cup	120 ml
2/3 cup	160 ml
3/4 cup	180 ml
1 cup (8 ounces)	240 ml
2 cups (1 pint)	480 ml
3 cups	720 ml
4 cups (1 quart)	1 litre
4 quarts (1 gallon)	3 3/4 litres

Dry Weights

U.S. Measurements	Metric Equivalents
1/4 ounce	7 grams
1/3 ounce	10 grams
1/2 ounce	14 grams
1 ounce	28 grams
1 1/2 ounces	42 grams
1 3/4 ounces	50 grams
2 ounces	57 grams
3 1/2 ounces	100 grams
4 ounces (1/4 pound)	114 grams
6 ounces	170 grams
8 ounces (1/2 pound)	227 grams
9 ounces	250 grams
16 ounces (1 pound)	464 grams

Temperatures

Fahrenheit	Celsius (Centigrade)
32°F (water freezes)	0°C
200°F	95°C
212°F (water boils)	100°C
250°F	120°C
275°F	135°C
300°F (slow oven)	150°C
325°F	160°C
350°F (moderate oven)	175°C
375°F	190°C
400°F (hot oven)	205°C
425°F	220°C
450°F (very hot oven)	230°C
475°F	245°C
500°F (extremely hot oven)	260°C

Length

U.S. Measurements	Metric Equivalents
1/8 inch	3 mm
1/4 inch	6 mm
3/8 inch	1 cm
1/2 inch	1.2 cm
3/4 inch	2 cm
1 inch	2.5 cm
1 1/4 inches	3.1 cm
1 1/2 inches	3.7 cm
2 inches	5 cm
3 inches	7.5 cm
4 inches	10 cm

Approximate Equivalents

1 kilo is slightly more than 2 pounds
1 litre is slightly more than 1 quart
1 centimeter is approximately 3/8 inch

Resources

Bridge Kitchenware Corporation
214 East 52nd Street
New York, NY 10022
(212) 838-6746

Cake Art
1512 5th Avenue
San Rafael, CA 94901
(415) 456-7773

Cost Plus
Stores Nationwide
(800) COST PLUS Mail Order Department

Crate & Barrel
Stores Nationwide
(800) 967-6696

King Arthur Flour
P.O. Box 876
Norwich, VT 05055-0876
(800) 827-6836 Mail Order Department

Lamalle Kitchenware
36 West 25th Street
New York, NY 10010
(800) 660-0750 Mail Order Department

Pier 1
Stores Nationwide
(800) 44-PIER1 Mail Order Department

Sugar 'n Spice
2965 Junipero Serra Boulevard
Daly City, CA 94014
(650) 994-4911

Sur La Table
84 Pine Street
Seattle, WA 98101
(206) 448-2244
(800) 243-0852 Mail Order Department

Sweet Celebrations
7009 Washington Avenue South
Edina, MN 55439
(800) 328-6722 Mail Order Department

Williams-Sonoma
Stores Nationwide
(800) 541-2233 Mail Order Department

Acknowledgments

Stephanie Greenleigh would like to express heartfelt thanks to the following people:

Susan Snider for her never-ending enthusiasm, optimism, and support; Claudia Breault for contributing creative recipe ideas, and for her help with the development and testing; Val Cipollone for her wonderful way with words and for her hand-holding through the book writing process; Teresa Retzlaff for being a great sounding board; Caroline Kopp for her eye and organizational skills; Jenna Mitchell for giving an eleven-year-old's perspective; Amy Nathan Weber for being a mentor and friend; my husband, John, for his unconditional love and support; and my children, Ian and Elise, for their patience and understanding in hearing me say repeatedly, "Just five more minutes."

Kathryn Kleinman wishes to extend her appreciation and thanks to the following people for their support on this project:

Teresa Retzlaff, studio manager and production coordinator, for her undivided attention to the details of this project; Caroline (Xena) Kopp, photography assistant extraordinaire; Jill Sorensen for her photo assistance and organizational help.

Thanks to Amanda Marcus, Lorraine Petersen, Mimi Lubberman, Lynn Scott of L. Scott & Co., and Luanne Blaich for the use of their beautiful linens, tableware, and accessories; Marcia and Patrick Maffei of Main Street Floragardens for supplying such wonderful flowers, and a special thanks to the O'Mearas of San Anselmo for the camellias.

Jennifer Barry Design would like to thank and acknowledge the following individuals for their help on this book project:

Special thanks to Kirsty Melville, publisher of Ten Speed Press, for her support and enthusiasm for the project, and to Lorena Jones, senior production editor, for her patience, help, and guidance.

Maria Hjelm for her enthusiastic support and marketing expertise, Val Cipollone for her astute editorial guidance, Emily Luchetti for her gracious editorial review, Barbara King for proofreading, Teresa Retzlaff for photo production support and archiving, Kristen Wurz for her design and project production assistance, Tom Johnson for his encouragement and production and technical assistance, and special thanks to Vicki Kalish of Williams-Sonoma for her guidance and support.

The project team wishes to acknowledge the following California establishments for their help with props and baking equipment: Williams-Sonoma, Crate & Barrel, and Pottery Barn, Corte Madera; Sur La Table, Tail of the Yak, and The Gardener, Berkeley; Smith & Hawken, Mill Valley; Main Street Floragardens and L. Scott & Co., San Anselmo; Chelsea Antiques, Petaluma; and Pine Street Papery, Sausalito.

Index

A

Apple blueberry turnovers, 68
Applesauce, pear, 87

B

Bars, ginger lime, 36
Blintzes, chocolate chip with strawberries, 90
Blueberry compote, 62, 63
Buttercream frosting, 49

C

Cake(s)
    chocolate amaretto torte, 59–60
    Fourth of July finale, 56–57
    mandarin orange angel, 55
    Meyer lemon pound, 44
Canapés, smoked trout and oat crisp, 96
Candied orange peel, 55
Challah French toast with pear applesauce, 87
Chantilly cream, 56, 57
Cherry and marzipan strudel, 71
Chocolate
    amaretto torte, 59–60
    banana muffins, 72
    chip blintzes with strawberries, 90
    glaze, 59, 60
    Meringue and chocolate kisses, 34
    Mexican chocolate and raspberry
        waffles, 89

Chocolate (continued)
    peanut butter lollipops, 40
    peppermint shortbread, 28
Coconut confetti cupcakes, 49
Coffeecake, marbled mocha pecan, 76
Compote, blueberry, 62, 63
Cookies
    chocolate peanut butter lollipops, 40
    chocolate peppermint shortbread, 28
    ginger lime bars, 36
    gingerbread, 27
    ischlers, 37
    linzer, 31
    meringue and chocolate kisses, 34
    New Year's fortune, 32
    pine nut wedding hearts, 38
    vanilla sugar, 22
Corncakes with tomato-orange salsa, 92
Cupcakes
    coconut confetti, 49
    royal hearts, 46

E

Eggs and batters
    challah French toast with pear
        applesauce, 87
    chocolate chip blintzes with
        strawberries, 90
    corncakes with tomato-orange salsa, 92

Eggs and batters (continued)
    eyes of the beholder, 81
    Father's Day frittata, 82
    Mexican chocolate and raspberry
        waffles, 89
    poppy seed pancakes, 84
Eyes of the beholder, 81

F

Father's Day frittata, 82
Fluffy pink icing, 46
Fourth of July finale, 56–57
French toast, challah with pear applesauce, 87
Frittata, Father's Day, 82
Frosting, buttercream, 49

G

Ginger lime bars, 36
Gingerbread cookies, 27
Glaze(s)
    chocolate, 59, 60
    rum, 75

I

Icing(s)
    fluffy pink, 46
    royal, 22
Ischlers, 37

J

Jeweled scones, 66

L

Lemon meringue tart with blueberry
    compote, 62–63
Linzer cookies, 31

M

Mandarin orange angel cake, 55
Marbled mocha pecan coffeecake, 76
Menu(s)
    for a baby shower, 95
    for a cookie decorating party, 21
Meringue and chocolate kisses, 34
Mexican chocolate and raspberry waffles, 89
Meyer lemon
    pound cake, 44
    syrup, 44
Muffins
    chocolate banana, 72
    peach-pocket cornmeal, 70

N

New Year's fortune cookies, 32

O

Orange peel, candied, 55

P

Pancakes, poppy seed, 84
Pastries
    apple blueberry turnovers, 68
    cherry and marzipan strudel, 71
Peach-pocket cornmeal muffins, 70
Pear applesauce, 87
Pine nut wedding hearts, 38
Poppy seed pancakes, 84
Potato cakes with shallots and thyme, 99

Q

Quick breads
    chocolate banana muffins, 72
    jeweled scones, 66
    marbled mocha pecan coffeecake, 76
    peach-pocket cornmeal muffins, 70
    tropical tea cake with rum glaze, 75

R

Rhubarb and strawberry country tart, 52
Roasted vegetable pinwheels, 98
Royal hearts cupcakes, 46
Royal icing, 22
Rum glaze, 75

S

Salsa, tomato-orange, 92
Scones, jeweled, 66
Shortbread, chocolate peppermint, 28
Smoked trout and oat crisp canapés, 96
Strudel, cherry and marzipan, 71

T

Tart(s)
    lemon meringue with blueberry
        compote, 62–63
    rhubarb and strawberry country, 52
    very berry, 51
Tea cake, tropical with rum glaze, 75
Tomato-orange salsa, 92
Torte, chocolate amaretto, 59–60
Tropical tea cake with rum glaze, 75
Turnovers, apple blueberry, 68

V

Vanilla sugar cookies, 22
Very berry tart, 51

W

Waffles, Mexican chocolate and raspberry, 89

Baked from the
Heart

Me • I'm Yours Forever • Love & Kisses • You're My
Love & Kisses • I Love You • You're Mine • Be My
es • I Love You • You're Mine • Be My Valentine • I
e • I'm Yours Forever • Love & Kisses • I Love You
One and Only • I Love You Truly • Kiss Me • Be My
Me • I'm Yours Forever • Love & Kisses • You're My
Love & Kisses • I Love You • You're Mine • Be My
es • I Love You • You're Mine • Be My Valentine • I
e • I'm Yours Forever • Love & Kisses • I Love You
One and Only • I Love You Truly • Kiss Me • Be My
Me • I'm Yours Forever • Love & Kisses • You're My
Love & Kisses • I Love You • You're Mine • Be My
es • I Love You • You're Mine • Be My Valentine • I
e • I'm Yours Forever • Love & Kisses • I Love You
One and Only • I Love You Truly • Kiss Me • Be My
Me • I'm Yours Forever • Love & Kisses • You're My
Love & Kisses • I Love You • You're Mine • Be My
es • I Love You • You're Mine • Be My Valentine • I

I Love You • You're Mine • Be My Valentine • Kiss
One and Only • I Love You Truly • I'm Yours Forever
Valentine • Kiss Me • I'm Yours Forever • Love & K
You're My One and Only • I Love You Truly • Kiss
Truly • I'm Yours Forever • Love & Kisses • You're M
I Love You • You're Mine • Be My Valentine • Kiss
One and Only • I Love You Truly • I'm Yours Forever
Valentine • Kiss Me • I'm Yours Forever • Love & K
You're My One and Only • I Love You Truly • Kiss
Truly • I'm Yours Forever • Love & Kisses • You're M
I Love You • You're Mine • Be My Valentine • Kiss
One and Only • I Love You Truly • I'm Yours Forever
Valentine • Kiss Me • I'm Yours Forever • Love & K
You're My One and Only • I Love You Truly • Kiss
Truly • I'm Yours Forever • Love & Kisses • You're M
I Love You • You're Mine • Be My Valentine • Kiss
One and Only • I Love You Truly • I'm Yours Forever
Valentine • Kiss Me • I'm Yours Forever • Love & K